Best Things Fathers Do

Best Things Fathers Do

IDEAS AND ADVICE FROM REAL-WORLD DADS

Will Glennon

Conari Press

First published in 2008 by Conari Press,
an imprint of Red Wheel/Weiser, LLC
With offices at:
500 Third Street, Suite 230
San Francisco, CA 94107
www.redwheelweiser.com

ISBN: 978-1-57324-355-1
Library of Congress Cataloging-in-Publication Data
Glennon, Will, 1949-
Best things fathers do : ideas and advice from real-world dads / Will Glennon.
p. cm.
ISBN 978-1-57324-355-1 (alk. paper)
1. Fathers. 2. Fatherhood. 3. Father and child. I. Title.
HQ756.G548 2008
649'.10851--dc22   2007048228

Cover and text design by Susan G. Schroeder.
Typeset in Adobe Garamond, P22 Garamouche, Kabel, KR Sports, KR Camping,
Providence Dingbats, Wiesbaden Swing, Parties and Ottofont.

Printed in Canada
TCP
10 9 8 7 6 5 4 3 2 1

Contents

Introduction

Why a book on the best things fathers can do? Because, in our age of equality at all cost, like it or not, fathers and mothers are still very, very different. Yes, things are starting to change, but that change is happening slowly. So we need to be honest and realistic—especially about something as crucially important as parenting.

In general, men tend to be very good at controlling their feelings. Most women may complain, with good cause, that we are too good at it. We are particularly good at "getting on with things" in the face of hardship, danger, pain, and turmoil. It is our training, our history, and even our mythology, weaned as we were on larger-than-life heroes stoically pushing forward to overcome enormous difficulties and crippling losses.

This skill, this ability to function effectively in the face of emotional pressure, has served us well, but it has also exacted a very high price. It has allowed us to create and accomplish out in the world with single-minded focus; but, largely unnoticed, it has also forced many of us to lose track of what is most important and precious, the reasons why we work so hard and what we are working for—our loved ones.

In homes all across the country, men are "getting on" with the business of living. But, as the statistics painfully demonstrate, in four out of five of those homes, they are doing it without the reassuringly deep comfort of a close emotional relationship with either their spouses or their children.

This book will hopefully give fathers some concrete tools (yeah, we love tools!) to build a close and powerful emotional connection that flows like a current of electricity between father and child. It is a most powerful thing and a most fragile one. It can be lost or interrupted abruptly, or it can persist over vast distances and time. It can make the difference between a life that is rich and full, and one that is empty and meaningless. It is one of our deepest desires as men, yet, for so many of us, it has proven to be painfully elusive.

Sadly, the tradition of fatherhood handed down to most of us is one of distance. And it is that distance of the father—physically and, much more important, emotionally—that is at the heart of the crisis. Paradoxically, however, it is the miracle of becoming a father that opens up for us the most inviting, most surprising, and most promising avenue for finding our way back to our hearts and souls. Fatherhood is a precious opportunity and we know it, even if we cannot comprehend or articulate why. It is something we feel in our bones. We want to understand it, to face the challenge and be found worthy; we know that there is something to it that can transform us if only we do it right, but often we don't even know how to begin.

Out of fear, out of ignorance, it is easiest to gravitate toward the patterns of fathering in which we were raised. From the birth of our first child, we tend to concede the role of comforter and nurturer to our wives and find ourselves removed from the child. The family dynamic becomes established, and we find ourselves somehow inexplicably "outside."

For most of us, it is not a good place to be, but we feel powerless to change it; we don't even have a vocabulary for how to talk about it. It is just a feeling, a very deep and painful feeling, but talking about our feelings is not something with which men are terribly comfortable. This distance, which is created slowly and silently, can no longer be tolerated. Somehow now—not tomorrow, not next year—we need to begin to forge a path back to our children, to discover how to create and maintain deep and strong emotional connections with them and ourselves.

I've also come to see that, when discussing fathering, there are no experts. There are only men who have tried to do their best and are willing to share their experience—their accomplishments and their failures, their heartaches and their joys, their confusion and their clarity.

There are no secret answers. Building and nurturing a father-child relationship requires the knowledge that it can be done, the commitment that it will be done, the persistence to keep on trying, and the courage to do whatever is necessary to make sure it does get done.

Like it or not, we are in the midst of a major economic, social, and cultural transition. The roles of men and women, and therefore the roles of mothers and fathers, are changing—and changing rapidly. These changes stem in part from new and often courageous choices being made by the emerging generations of women and men, and also in part from the very impersonal and inexorable economic shifts taking place.

What we want, need, and expect from our most intimate relationships are being reexamined and redefined as we go. At the same time, women are moving into the workplace at an astonishing rate, out of both choice and necessity. The result is a boiling cauldron of change in the most vulnerable places in our lives. One of the most visible casualties is the tragedy of the absent father—whether in another city, another home, another room, or simply always at work.

Change is difficult and painful—painful because the ways of the past now appear sadly inadequate, painful because what should replace the ways of the past is not at all clear, and painful because, regardless of the wounds, constraints, injustices, or inadequacies of the "old way," they also had benefits, particularly the comfort of familiarity. Painful or not, these changes are upon us. Whether we applaud, fear, or resent them no longer matters; they are here and we must deal with them.

The distance our fathers accepted as natural and appropriate is now threatening to unravel the very social fabric of parenting. The simplistic response to this by many men is an angry rejection of the "old ways," most often expressed in some variation of "I won't make the mistakes my father made."

It is true that, if we are smart enough, courageous enough, persistent enough, and vigilant enough, we won't make the same mistakes our fathers made—we will make our own mistakes. But before we toss out our fathers with last year's calendar, it may help to remember that they grew up in another time and, in a very real sense, pioneered a new era.

This is more true today than it has ever been. Television, jet airplanes, telephones, copiers and fax machines, personal computers, the list goes on and on—all are essential fixtures in our lifetime that did not exist when most of our fathers were growing up. And, of course, their most important lessons about fathering came from their fathers, many of whom were born in the nineteenth century. We can turn our backs in hurt and anger at the fathering style we were handed, but that would be wrong, it would be wasteful, and it would be disrespectful.

Despite what anger or sorrow we may have at how we were fathered, we can't afford to discard the hard-won lessons of our fathers carelessly. We need to take the best of what they gave us as we plot a course toward a new kind of fathering—one built on strong bonds of love, one that is expansive and courageous, and one that will bring us back into the richness of a deep emotional connection with our children.

If we ask people to select words to describe positively what it means to be a mother, invariably they come up with such terms as nurturing, compassionate, caring, and comforting. For fathers, the words are protector, provider, responsible, dependable, hardworking, and problem-solving. Those characteristics fit well with our culturally projected father images, like those portrayed in *Leave It to Beaver* and *Father Knows Best*. In these television households, fathers Ward and Tom are portrayed as kind and understanding men who are primarily problem-solvers—that is, men who diffuse and avoid emotional situations by presenting real-world solutions.

If we combine these characteristic mother and father qualities, we end up with an impressive résumé for good parenting. Traditionally, however, these characteristics have been divided up by gender, with women assigned the internal or emotional tasks and men assigned the external tasks of dealing with the outside world. This division has deep roots in our history but, for better and for worse, it is rapidly deteriorating. The radically changing nature of what it means to be a man or a woman is not news, but it is a constant source of challenge and opportunity.

Over the past thirty years, it's become obvious that women are no longer content to live within the boundaries of traditional gender roles that severely limit the scope and magnitude of their dreams. What is now becoming evident is that men also cannot continue to play out their appointed roles blindly without increasingly disastrous consequences to their own emotional health and that of their children.

When we examine social evolution in more detail, at least some of the reason for the urgency in dealing with the changing role of fathers begins to emerge. For, although the traditional roles of mothers and fathers may appear clear and defined, in practice, they were never as stark or as isolating as they appear to us today.

Until relatively recently—the past 100 years or so—men and women carried out their roles in close and constant contact with each other and with their children, whether on a small farm or running a small business or shop. Indeed, for most of our history, men and women worked side by side—undertaking different tasks, but performing them in a manner that involved continuous interaction, feedback, and assistance.

Dad was indeed the protector and provider, but he was also right there, downstairs in the shop or out in the field preparing it for next season's crop. More often than not, Dad was there every day for the noontime meal, as well as for breakfast and supper, and the opportunities (and indeed, obligation) for children to spend time with Dad by helping out in the fields or in the store were frequent.

Fathers fulfilled their role in frequent daily contact with their children, and that contact nurtured the kinds of emotional connections that can only come with the investment of time. That began to change in our great-grandfathers' and grandfathers' time, as swelling waves of refugees fled the poverty of the countryside to find work in the factories and offices of cities around the world.

Increasingly, this new economic reality found fathers leaving home early in the morning and not returning until late at night. The thread of daily contact with their children was lost, as was the constant contact between husband and wife. The division of labor between men and women, which in the past had existed as a relatively intimate partnership, became a division in time and place as well. Fathers were increasingly removed from the home, and mothers became more isolated from the workaday world. This everyday enforced distance became the true rupture with the past.

It is impossible to overemphasize the importance of this change. For, in building and maintaining close personal relationships, time is a key ingredient, and it is our time with our fathers when we were growing up, as well as with our children as they are growing up, that has been taken away from us.

We don't live our lives in isolation from these larger social conditions. We don't make the rules, and we aren't even given a decent map to follow. The vast flow of history, with its wave after wave of social and economic change, has established the conditions under which our lives must be lived. We would like to believe that we have more control over our lives, but time and experience prove to us again and again that the most we can do is choose how we will respond to the circumstances we are given.

Fathers today, young and old, have been dealt a very difficult hand. Because of the massive social and economic migrations over the past 100 years, as a group, we have been deprived of the daily close contact with our fathers and our children that many of our grandfathers and most of their fathers enjoyed.

Separated from both our fathers and our children, we have been cut off from the heart of the fathering traditions of the past and have been handed a decidedly garbled message about how we should go about being good fathers today.

1

Jump in Immediately with Both Feet!

Fathers are different from mothers. It's so obvious that we don't even stop to think about what the difference really means. The relationship of a mother and her child develops quite literally from the inside out. For nine months, the mother and her child are together in a physical symbiosis that defies comprehension. On the most elemental level, they share in the miracle of creation, and the day of birth is but the first important milestone in their already-established connection.

Get inside and stay inside

Fathers come to their children from the outside from the very beginning. We can participate in the progress of our wives' pregnancies, we can place our hands in strategic spots to feel the kicks and jabs, we can listen to the swooshing heartbeat through a stethoscope, and now, thanks to the marvels of technology, we can watch videos of our child floating gently in an embryonic world. But our experience is always filtered; no matter how we participate, fundamentally we remain on the outside. Our first real contact with our child is when we cradle our newborn in our arms.

In some profound way, our biological placement in the process of birth mirrors the challenges we will face throughout our children's lives. For most mothers, the primary struggle of parenthood is stepping back far enough to allow the child the room to grow and develop. The challenge for most men, on the other hand, is coming in close enough so that we can build a strong and lasting bond.

As surprising as it may seem, the most crucial time to impact your future relationship with your children dramatically is in the first few years of their lives. This is a time when love and commitment are communicated on the most basic level. A child's infancy is a time of tremendous leverage. The foundation we establish—or fail to establish—will either allow us to build and maintain a close emotional connection with relative ease, or will instill a distance that will make our later efforts more difficult.

The birth of his first child is a pivotal moment in a father's life. It is a time when he must choose—whether he wants to or not—the emotional orbit from which he will do his fathering. The newborn offers a father an opportunity, a doorway back to the emotional world. This is an extraordinary, and tragically, often-overlooked possibility. If we choose to open ourselves as widely as possible, to meet our children in the frighteningly vulnerable place from which they begin, it can reunite us with a time and place when we too felt completely defenseless, completely exposed, and completely vulnerable. In this manner, it can broaden us and make us wiser.

Pulled together at the moment of birth, father and child will either forge an unbreakable connection or begin drifting apart. This opportunity is fragile and fleeting, existing for only a brief moment before the mundaneness of daily life returns in full force. Once this time has passed, crossing the distance becomes more and more difficult. It can be done—distance can always be erased where the love and desire are strong enough—but it becomes more and more difficult as time passes.

Because of this, becoming a father is a precious and sacred time in a man's life, but unfortunately, it is rarely acknowledged as such. We arrive at this moment almost completely unprepared—no wise, elderly male relative takes us aside and impresses upon us the importance of seizing the chance for deep bonding. Too often, the moment passes without our even understanding the opportunity that is already slipping away.

Do your homework

Fathering is one of men's most important and certainly most difficult undertakings, yet most of us enter into fatherhood with only the most rudimentary concept of what is expected of us. From any rational perspective, fatherhood is a great mystery. We live in a society that prizes preparation, training, and expertise for almost everything, but leaves us woefully unprepared for the single most challenging task of all. The more information we have, the more clear it becomes how vitally important the father/child relationship is, yet the patterns of our society appear simply to assume that men have only a ceremonial role in the shaping of their children's lives. We become fathers with stunning ignorance. And unfortunately, we are smack in the middle of the period of greatest nescience—our child's infancy—before we ever realize just how ill-prepared we are.

Why did no one warn us? Although, in most cases, our initiation into the bewildering world of fatherhood was not something done to us intentionally, at the time, it certainly seems like a peculiarly cruel joke.

For the most part, as boys, we were rarely included in any infant-care activities and were unwelcome when adults talked about parenting issues. When a little brother or sister came along, we may have been placed ceremonially on a well-cushioned chair and allowed to "hold" the child for a few minutes, but for all practical purposes, the message came through loud and clear that, when Mom (occasionally with the assistance of Big Sister) was dealing with the babies, the best all-around strategy was for us to be somewhere else—preferably harmlessly entertaining ourselves.

Nor did many of us have any real models for what a father is supposed to be. Our fathers, all too often, were not around. Either they were at work all day and sometimes until well into the evening (so were too tired when they came home to really interact), or they were not even in the same household. And when they were around, they were generally uninvolved in the down-and-dirty parenting tasks. How many of us over the age of twenty-five can remember our fathers doing laundry or picking us up from school? On the day-to-day level, most of us grew up in a world where the nuts-and-bolts of parenting was done by women. Our chins and bottoms were wiped, our food prepared and served, and our scratches and bruises attended to and kissed away mainly by Mom, but often with help from Grandma, a handful of aunts, and occasionally a big sister.

Our experience of fathering was usually restricted to predictably narrow areas: Dad firmly held the expectations that you were supposed to live up to; Dad lowered the boom when you really screwed up and was the one you went to when you had a big problem that needed solving; and every now and then, he was the one who would take you on a special outing.

Given this cultural background, it is certainly understandable that we would arrive at the gates of fatherhood woefully unprepared. What is difficult to understand is how, as a society, we could somehow silently conspire to bring one man after another to the brink of the most important job in his lifetime not only without preparing him, but without even talking to him about it.

While this profound lack of preparedness is all too often a reality in the world of fatherhood, in the world of work, it never happens. Imagine for a minute being relatively young and a pretty good salesman, though still fairly inexperienced in the working world. The president of your multinational corporation calls you up to tell you that you've just been promoted to chief financial officer. After a momentary fleeting fantasy of the big raise and leap in status, you no doubt conclude that this guy is nuts. You are no more prepared to be chief financial officer than you are to do the brain surgery your boss obviously needs!

Although we dedicate the vast resources of our educational system to preparing us for the tasks we will face later in life, not only do we not teach our sons the skills they will need to be good fathers, we act as though fathering skills are instinctual or biological and will simply emerge automatically, like a new mother's breast milk.

It doesn't work that way. When an infant cries, nursing mothers often experience a responsive leaking of breast milk; there are, after all, some powerful survival-of-the-species factors at work in that relationship. Unfortunately, a father does not automatically know what is wrong or what needs to be done when a baby cries. Fathering is a skill that must be learned and, for the most part, is one we don't bother to pass on.

Men also don't have the ritual support that so many women have. When a baby is born, grandmothers, sisters, and female friends all come out of the woodwork to hover and coo over the new addition, while the exhausted mom is alternately encouraged into her new child-care duties and pampered and fussed over by the temporary support team. It is a momentous occasion to cross over that unspoken borderline between being one of the women to being one of the mothers. It is observed and acknowledged in hundreds of small ways, from baby showers to visits from all the female relatives. It is not as though anyone decided or intended to exclude the new father, but the focus is clearly and specifically on mother and child—Dad is somewhere unobtrusive in the background.

The minute a man faces the most momentous change he will ever encounter, he is pressed by tradition, by circumstances, and often by his own fear into assuming a quietly receding position. While reason and compassion dictate that the new father should be ritually welcomed and as emotionally propped up and supported at this crucial juncture as the new mother is, he is often ignored, left to deal with his insecurities with stoic silence or nervous bravado.

So, until we as a society finally figure out that being a father deserves the energy and preparation we can give it, the least we can do is dedicate ourselves to a rapid trajectory of on-the-job learning, and that includes talking to every good father role model we can find.

Seize the opportunity to become an emotional warrior

One of the secrets about good fathering is that it is primarily about feelings. His child's infancy is the time in a man's life when he is given the opportunity to return, fully and completely, to his heart. After spending much of the previous two or three decades learning how to conquer and control our feelings in order to operate effectively in the world, fatherhood presents us with the sudden and scary opportunity to become reacquainted with that inner part of ourselves.

Life has a way of delivering lessons in a form that we can handle. Reintroducing a man to his emotional side can, as most women will certainly attest, be a very tall order. But when the teacher is his very own tiny, helpless infant, the process can be simple, painless, and a source of immeasurable joy, as many of the men I have spoken with can attest. Cradled in the security of mutual, unconditional love, it is the single safest emotional relationship most men will ever encounter.

Interacting with an infant is the most introductory course in deep emotions imaginable. Add to that the fact that we are starting with the real basics—infants need to be held, fed, stroked, talked to, played with, bathed, and comforted—and you get to practice all you want without fear of rejection. You know going in that every touch, every funny face, every hug, every tickle, every time you say "I love you," every time you watch your child's latest accomplishment with wonder, your child is blossoming with your love.

A child's infancy is a very physical time, so dive in and enjoy it. From feeding, diapering, and bathing to tying on those tiny booties and trying to direct a flailing hand down a shirt sleeve, it is a time when your child needs you to perform the most rudimentary and essential tasks. Despite the traditional gender allocation of these duties—with the single exception of breast-feeding—they are neither particularly mysterious nor difficult, and fathers aren't any less suited to them than mothers are. And they present us with daily opportunities to nurture and strengthen the bonds with our children.

Infancy is truly a time of miracles. Your child's mind and body is growing at such a dramatic rate that he or she is a new person every day. The tiny hand that waves aimlessly around one day is purposefully (and gleefully) dropping peas off the high chair tray the next. Overnight, all the gurgling and lip-smacking turn into distinct sounds, then words, then demands. The helpless, wiggling infant, whose sole method of getting anything accomplished is to cry, transforms before your very eyes (and long before you are properly prepared) into a marvel of locomotion, knocking down anything and everything in its path and turning any bottom shelf into complete disarray.

Although babyhood may appear to be a period of great fragility, in fact it's a rough-and-tumble time of constant creation and discovery. No father worth his salt would allow his child to disappear on a long journey of exploration unaccompanied, which is exactly what happens if you don't make a conscious effort to dive into fatherhood—by becoming a master of the quick diaper change, learning the intricate flight patterns for spooning mashed peas into an anxiously circling mouth while enthusiastically babbling nonsense, locating every ticklish spot on your child's body, and reading *A Fly Went By* 700 times without appearing to lose interest in how it turns out.

As new fathers, we enter this moment of our lives profoundly unprepared. If we have a supportive wife, if we can find the courage to overcome our fears and insecurities, if we are lucky enough to have male friends to encourage us in the process, we have the opportunity to begin again—to participate actively in the miraculous process of creating an individual. And in so doing, we are taken back and allowed to relive, re-create, and refashion those parts of our own being that no longer serve us well.

It seems important to start with this, the deepest truth of fathering—that your children can take you back and can set you free. From here, we can begin to create the intricate web of connections that bind us to our children. It is never too early to begin but, because of the miracle of love, it is also never too late.

If we are failing our children, it is not because we don't love them, not because we don't want to be the best fathers we can possibly be, but rather because the rules have all changed and no one bothered to tell us, much less give us a copy of the new rule book. We feel, as one man said, "a little like a character in a *Twilight Zone* episode. One day I just woke up in another dimension, where no matter what I tried to do, it turned out to be the wrong thing."

At the heart of the problem is our collective difficulty in dealing with things emotional, an inhibition that robs our children of one of the most essential resources necessary for building a healthy, self-confident personality—our heartfelt, feeling presence.

Under normal circumstances, our strength as problem-solvers would rise to the occasion. However, growing up male has ill-prepared us for dealing with this one—we have a very limited emotional vocabulary and little experience, much of it negative, in emotional dialog. It is one of the problems that helped get us here in the first place. Often, we remain at arm's length from our children, because we fear we don't have the skills to do it right. We inherited this lack of emotional facility from our fathers, who themselves struggled mightily in the emotional realm.

Because we, too, for the most part were raised to follow a similar code of emotional silence, we find ourselves untrained, unsupported, unsure, and uneasy in the crucial task of emotionally nurturing our children. But this is precisely what we are being called upon to do.

It is always difficult to make a change, because it's new, because it's different, but mostly because it implies that the way we used to do things was all wrong. In practice, things don't really work that way. What was appropriate forty years ago may not be appropriate today. Largely because we have had virtually no training for what is being asked of us, this particular transition for men is even more difficult and confusing than most. The temptation is to long for the illusory comfort of some past golden era. But fathering is too important to treat so cavalierly. We must face who we are and where we are right now. Like it or not, whereas our fathers pioneered a new technological era, we now blaze a trail on the frontier of human relationships.

There is a scene in one of the *Star Trek* movies in which Captain Kirk says: "The situation is grim and the odds of succeeding are slim—sounds like fun." This pokes fun at the swashbuckling nature of the early *Star Trek* TV show, but it is also speaking to the fearless adventurer within each of us. Historically, it wasn't that long ago that, when fathers were called upon to be protectors, it was in deadly serious physical combat. Whether it was battling a group of marauding bandits, a rival tribe, or an organized army of invaders, fathers fought to protect their children.

This is a characteristic of fathering that we are comfortable with; it is the most visible and receives the most attention. Along with the ability to solve problems and resolve conflicts, a father's role as protector is something we as a society have traditionally appreciated; it is perhaps the most dramatic manifestation of father love.

But in the final analysis, the most important quality of a good father at this point in history is the capacity to communicate and share deep feelings with our children. That's because the heart of fathering is fathering from the heart. It is about how our children feel—about us, about their own self-esteem and sense of self-worth, about the value and importance of their unique personalities. It is about how effective we are at helping our children understand and embrace their own feelings. These are the most precious gifts that we can give our children, the resources that will allow them to live rich and full lives.

Although fathering on the day-to-day level is often about doing—something for which most of our fathers prepared us very well—on the fundamental level, it is almost exclusively about feeling. This crucial truth is easy for us to dismiss or ignore. Because it seems to come more naturally to us and because we are better at it, we tend to elevate the role of father as teacher to the position of highest importance. We focus on the need to teach our children good, effective behavior so that, whatever they do in life, they will do it well.

As men, we tend to define ourselves by the work we do. I am a carpenter, a lawyer, a manager, a mechanic. But obviously, we are much more than that. We are fathers, husbands, lovers, sons; we are members of a broader community; we are individuals with our own beliefs and convictions. Ultimately, when we really want someone to understand our uniquely individual perspective, we say, "I feel very strongly about this."

Once again, we are being called to fight for our children, only this time the battle is in a decidedly different arena and will not be waged with muscle and weapons. We can draw on the courage and determination of the generations of fathers that have gone before us, but we must develop new and different skills. This time, the enemy is all the nameless and faceless pressures that push us away from a deep connection with our children. Our battle is about feelings—ours and theirs. Ultimately, it is about becoming conversant enough and comfortable enough with our own emotions to be able to receive and nurture the feelings of our children.

This, then, is our challenge: to become emotional warriors, to return to the heart of fathering. We must approach this challenge with determination and the conviction that, by focusing our efforts here, at the very core of what it means to be a father, we can rewrite the rules and transform the landscape of parenting.

Communicating our love to our children and acknowledging their importance in our lives is an undertaking of enormous significance—for our children, for our own well-being, and for generations of fathers to come. Historically and socially, we are conditioned to put aside our feelings in order to fight. The purpose for which we must fight is to become fully engaged with our feelings in order to reinstate ourselves in our proper place in our children's lives. The effort requires courage and determination, for this is new territory, and we will no doubt make mistakes.

It is also an endeavor that still, despite the pioneering work of many fathers, runs counter to what is expected and accepted. "Out there," in the world, the business culture still expects us to exist primarily for the sake of doing our jobs. The man who is perceived as being more concerned about spending time with his children than worrying about his job is still looked down on by many as ineffectual or, more bluntly, as a wimp.

There is a subculture in the working world made up of men who have chosen to sacrifice any and all genuine human interactions for the sake of business success. Many in this group rise to important positions precisely because they are willing to sacrifice everything, including their relationships with their wives and children, to succeed. Unfortunately, these are sometimes the very people with whom the rest of us must somehow deal; and, all too often, the only way they know to defend their own choices is to be absolutely cutthroat in their dealings with any man unwilling to make the same sacrifices.

Make no mistake, this is and will continue to be a substantial obstacle. For a man who has chosen to sacrifice family life for the sake of his job to see another man refuse to make that sacrifice and still be an effective worker starkly reveals the unnecessarily tragic folly of such a decision. Because of this, there will be plenty of men out there who will go out of their way to make it more difficult for you.

It takes considerable courage to walk through that wall of fire and remain committed to being a feeling man. Even in the best of work environments, it is rare that a man will find true support for career sacrifices made in the name of good fathering.

In some sense, the external obstacles we must confront will be the easiest to manage. They are, at least, easy to identify, and we can fall back on our more familiar male problem-solving skills to get around them. The internal obstacles are more difficult both to identify and to master.

One of the thorniest issues stems from the sad truth that, in today's world, men are not rewarded for being good fathers, but rather for making lots of money and wielding lots of power. We may deplore the heartless, superficial nature of this pecking order, but can we resist the sirens' call? Like those mythical beauties whose songs lured sailors onto the deadly rocks, the attraction of status is tempting. Raised on the importance of competition and striving for excellence, can we refuse to compete in the arena? We know it is distorted and out of balance, but we also know that this is where the public rewards are handed out.

This is a delicate issue. Working and achieving are important; they are necessary to being a good provider. And, if we are lucky, it can be through our work that we make a contribution to and thus our mark in the world. The trick is to accomplish what we need to without crashing on the rocks of total self-absorption.

For many of us, the most difficult obstacle will be our fear of our own emotions. In his first inaugural address, Franklin D. Roosevelt reminded Americans that "the only thing we have to fear is fear itself." For a man, it is much easier to rally to that call to courage when the danger is from the outside; when the danger appears to well up within our own hearts, however, we are not at all sure we have the resources to persist.

Our cultural stereotypes portray women as too focused on emotions, and men as largely oblivious to the world of feelings. The theme recurs with as much regularity in domestic quarrels as it does in bestselling books and comedy routines. That's because, as much as it is a gross overstatement, it is also substantially true.

If we, as fathers, are to make this journey, we must admit up front how difficult it is for most of us to be willing to feel—much less express—the full range of emotions we have kept bottled up so successfully. After all, it's tough to become a skilled practitioner at anything if you can't at least begin with a clear picture of your own weaknesses.

A good part of the problem is of our own making. For a world of reasons that psychologists would be more than happy to explain, most of us developed quite early the habit of avoiding our emotions by simply repressing them. We shove them down into some dark space, where we hope they will stay—and they do for the time being. But emotions have their own rhythm and cannot be ignored so easily, at least not permanently. Eventually, they come out—one way or another.

The net effect of tamping them down is much like over-inflating a tire—the ride gets more and more jarring, and the pressure mounts to the point where you cringe at every bump in anticipation of a blowout. After years of allowing the pressure to build, it can take considerable courage just to be willing to acknowledge and examine the feelings that have been bottled up for so long, and even more courage to actually feel and express them.

Men tend to be pretty good at analysis, but it helps if what we are analyzing can be seen, touched, measured, and examined. Emotions are more like energy than anything else. Although we can see their effects, we can't see emotions themselves. They pulse, vibrate, and crackle like an overloaded transformer, but we cannot get our hands on them. We can sense their tremendous power, but it cannot be controlled or harnessed. Entering the world of our own emotions, therefore, can be every bit as frightening as the idea of holding 10,000 volts of electricity in our hands.

Ironically, one of the miracles of our emotions is that they allow us to experience things vastly beyond the limited capacities of our physical selves. Our emotions, our extraordinary capacity to feel, constitute the expansive energy that makes up our essential identity—the core of who we are. Everything we are flows from that source—what we want and need in life, our desires, our hopes, our dreams. In a very profound way, each of us is truly what we feel.

Once we are willing to enter this world without reservation, we discover (to our great relief) that, as overwhelming as it can feel, it is only a feeling. Not only can we survive, we can thrive as we become more and more comfortable in this venue. And for this we should be thankful, because the world of our emotions is a vastly complex and intricate one of which we can no longer remain ignorant.

We need to become experts—to learn how to harness this extraordinary energy and understand what we are feeling and why we are experiencing those particular feelings. We need to learn how to describe and communicate our feelings in a way that others can understand. These skills are critical, because they are the tools with which we will build a strong and lasting connection to our children.

If we imagine our emotions as high-voltage electricity pulsing within us, all that is missing is the connection—the circuitry—that allows that energy to flow back and forth between us and our children. Without this connection, we are like a power tool that is unplugged. We can be present physically, interacting with our children, but the powerful flow of our vital energy is missing—an emotional blackout. It's like trying to drill a hole with a disconnected power drill—something may be happening, but it won't be what you are trying to accomplish.

Promote and encourage real family values

Face it: fathers are not getting the clearest of messages these days. Mostly, we are unsure of how to proceed. The message that comes through the loudest and resonates the strongest is that we must be protectors and providers. The image of the father as protector and provider is so deeply ingrained in our cultural heritage that it feels as though failing at this means risking our identity as men. And so we throw ourselves into the role with fierce determination, as though fulfilling this aspect of our identity as fathers were enough.

For most men, it is when our children are very young that we need to work the hardest. We may be new on the job, often insecure about our work identity. We need to put in long hours to become better at what we do, to become more valuable to the company, or to be recognized as an important employee. Out of fear, insecurity, and need, we put in long hours at work and have precious little time left to spend with our children.

Before we know it, the tiny creatures we brought home from the hospital are crawling, then walking, then running to greet us at the door each evening. And as they grow, so too do their needs—clothes, shoes, medical bills, braces, piano lessons, judo classes. This is also frequently the time in our careers when we have greater opportunities for advancement, and that, of course, means even more attention to work, more hours spent on the job, and more work being brought home to intrude on the few hours available for our children. Even men who start out intending to do things differently find themselves in the provider trap.

Because we love our children so much, we want desperately to be good providers, and so we work very hard at it. Then suddenly, we find ourselves deep into the middle years of our children's youth, at a distance we never planned for or wanted. We find ourselves on the outside looking in at their lives—their rhythms and schedules—much of which is constructed without concern for our presence, because, in truth, it is very difficult to assure them we will be there. We try. We try to get to the soccer match, to show up at the parent/teacher night, to get home early so we can play catch, but it is very difficult. They learn to stop counting on us to be there in order not to feel the sharp sting of disappointment, and we end up feeling left out.

Time is important, whether we want it to be or not. The more time we spend working, the more energy we pour into our jobs, the more all-consuming they can become. Without our ever intending it, work can assume a larger and larger piece of our self-image. It can absorb so much of our identity that it becomes the only thing from which we can derive satisfaction, the only place we feel appreciated. If we are particularly good at our jobs, they can also become the place where our accomplishments are honored and acknowledged—the center of our feelings of self-worth.

The less time we spend at home, the less familiar it becomes. We lose track of what is going on in our children's lives. We don't know the names of their friends or their enemies, what they like or what bothers them. It can be very disconcerting to listen to an explanation of an event of crucial importance to your six-year-old and realize that you know neither the landscape nor the actors.

This lack of involvement, like a small crack in the windshield, can widen and worsen if left untended, as our children begin to express their anger over our absence in any number of creative ways that are guaranteed to make time spent at home even less enjoyable. This can become just one more pressure pushing us farther away, or it can be the wake-up call that something needs to change. Fathers need to be alert to all the pressures pushing them into a one-dimensional role and then resist like mad!

Unfortunately, we don't all have the ability to restructure our work life unilaterally and still be able to pay the bills, but we are all faced with the same dilemma. For the most part, the very job opportunities that allow us to provide for our children threaten to pull us so far apart from them that we may lose the very thing we are working so hard to maintain—our family. And until recently, there was very little acknowledgment of this issue by employers.

Balancing work and family life is a very real and difficult problem with no simple solutions. We cannot return en masse to the days of small shops and single-family farms; those options are no longer economically viable on any large scale. Nor can we simply quit our jobs or abandon our children. Broadening the awareness and sensitivity of employers to the problems fathers face and demanding and getting flexible work schedules, and more realistic paternity leave and child-care policies will take considerable time and effort.

It feels for all the world as if we are stuck between a rock and a hard place, being slowly ground into pieces. And recent changes in our economic landscape are not making things any easier. The growing pains of a truly international economy have forced a wave of corporate downsizing, which in real language means that fewer good jobs are available; and the lucky ones who have those jobs are being increasingly called upon to work longer hours. As fathers, we have to fight in an intensely stressful job market to find work that will enable us to provide for our children; and, at the same time, if we are successful, we must somehow resist the job pressures that pull us farther and farther away from them.

Given all these factors, being a father at this moment in history is no picnic. We are understandably expected to provide for our children and attacked as deadbeat dads if we fail. At the same time, we end up sacrificing precious time with our children in order to provide for them, and then come under criticism for not being with them enough.

For many men, it feels like an impossible situation—and there are no easy fixes on the horizon. Yet this is the hand we have been dealt, and the stakes are far too high to walk away without trying. For, as great a social tragedy as the absent father has become, it is so much more a personal tragedy for our children, who are growing up without our support and nurturing, and a loss for those of us who are severed from the miracle of our children's lives.

We need to begin to redefine fathering in a way that makes sense at this point in our history so that it can provide the kind of reassuring comfort and strength for our children that it should. We need to search for ways around the seemingly impossible bind we find ourselves in so that, when we work, it is for a deeper purpose and, when we are home with our children, it is as the fathers we want to be. In order to do all this, we need to look a little closer at the factors that keep us separated from our children.

One of the best things fathers can do is start supporting and advocating for a more family-friendly work environment. This means both moving toward a more European system with more time off, and encouraging and taking real family-leave time.

Don't fall prey to the addicted-to-work syndrome

Even if men are properly prepared in the diaper-and-bottle department, we are still woefully unready for the sudden and dramatic realization of the awesome responsibility we have just taken on. You can do what you can ahead of time to prepare yourself, but nothing will make you ready for the impact of the feelings that are suddenly unleashed. This is your child, whom it is your responsibility to protect. You must make sure that nothing bad ever befalls him or her.

If there is any instinctive "father response" bred into men, most fathers would probably agree that it is the overpowering urge to protect at all costs the helpless infant that has suddenly become their charge. It is a rare father who has not experienced that powerful rush of adrenaline at the door to fatherhood, and the strength of those feelings raises the odds dramatically. What prior to your first child's birth was a logical understanding of the extra financial burden you were about to undertake, coupled with a vague notion of the time and energy commitment that would be required, is suddenly elevated to life-and-death issues—this is your child, and your sense of duty and responsibility expands almost beyond bearing.

Ironically, men's response to this protective impulse often leads them into a series of actions and reactions that draws them farther and farther away from the real tasks of fathering. Becoming a father is almost always frightening, and, when our sensitivities are raised so quickly and dramatically at the birth of our first child, often our initial response is near panic. Right when the arrival of our child has opened up emotional channels into the most vulnerable part of our hearts, we are suddenly placed in a situation in which we don't understand the procedures, much less the rules, and we are hit with a very real and practical expansion of our job description.

Add to that a wife who is, at the very least, temporarily out of the job market, and you have a prescription for a large sack of emotional and financial burdens that men often find hard to carry. But carry it we must, because it is our job, because we feel it is our responsibility as men, even if we are not at all sure we can measure up. It can be a terrifying beginning, because if we can't protect our new family from even the insecurity caused by its inception, we have failed before we even begin. In the midst of this swirl of fear, our immediate response is to grab hold of anything that appears solid and, more often than not, that means putting up at least a pretense of being strong. We want our wives and babies to feel our protective strength, not our quivering insecurity. And often, that's what our wives want from us, too.

Given all these realities, a new father can end up, not by design but by circumstance, withdrawing at precisely the moment when he should be reaching out. Feeling unimportant, left out, and frightened, he is apt to retreat into silent stoicism—feeling the enormous load of his newborn responsibility, but having no apparent support or acknowledgment from the outside and no ready avenue to relieve his burden.

This terror of the burden we have assumed is often just the first subtle push of what all too easily can propel a new father into a trajectory that takes him away from his child. By shutting down instead of opening up, by pulling away toward the seductive safety of isolation instead of stepping forward into the frightening no-man's-land of an infant's very raw needs, a new father can unintentionally establish an emotional distance between himself and his child that will be difficult to bridge.

To some new fathers, witnessing the power of the mother/child connection can be so dramatic that they retreat out of respect rather than fear. Add to that the return these days to breast- rather than bottle-feeding, and men can find themselves in the very uncomfortable position of not being able to satisfy their crying baby's very real needs. Whether out of respect, fear, or circumstance, the result is the same—the entrenchment of distance between father and child.

Ironically, our collective mythology about women being intuitive and "natural-born" mothers often contributes to nudging new fathers away from forming a strong emotional bond with their newborn children early on. Many new mothers express their own insecurities about mothering by being overly attentive and focused on their infant. This can come across to an often nervous and baffled father as a possessive and near exclusive takeover of all the nurturing and comforting roles. We men frequently contribute to this unconscious takeover because, after all, we are already feeling inept, and it suits our need for security to imagine that our wives really are "naturally" good at this sort of thing.

Mom takes maternity leave and spends her time in intensive training sessions. Fathers, on the other hand, rarely take parental leave and begin almost immediately to see and interact with their child in limited and repetitive ways. As a result, the new mother quickly learns to interpret the cries and body language of her tiny infant. She becomes, through trial and error, in tune with the feelings and expressions of this emerging little person, while Dad lags behind.

When Dad is late in picking up the infant's signs of need, Mom, who by now understands the signals, steps in to take over. Because children, like adults, naturally gravitate toward those who provide them with the nurture and comfort they need, before we know what has happened, our babies are crawling to Mommy for comfort, our toddlers always want to go with Mommy—and we're left wondering what happened. The cumulative effect is the establishment of a polarization in which Mom assumes virtually all the roles of comforting and nurturing and Dad recedes into the distance—outside the orbit of the deepest emotional connections.

At the same time we are losing out on precious opportunities to bond with our babies. The first days of fatherhood are often taken up by myriad burdensome tasks, interrupted constantly. Whatever schedule we used to observe is blown to pieces. Waking, sleeping, eating, even limited conversation with your wife are now suddenly and completely at the unconscious whim of your child. Most men find themselves in the position of trying to smooth over all the interactions with the outside world, leaving mother and child within a hastily (and imperfectly) fashioned cocoon of protection.

Usually, this means that the careful division of labor with which you and your wife had become comfortable is shattered by the unbelievable level of attention a newborn requires. While Mom redirects her energy toward caring for your child, you find yourself picking up the slack at the grocery store, in trips to the cleaners, in kitchen duty, and in any number of small but time-consuming tasks that must get done.

It is an exhausting time, made even more so by the predictable late-night alarm clock of your hungry child's cry. If the fatigue is being balanced by the emergence of deep emotional bonds between you and your child, it is only of passing consequence. But if the exhaustion is experienced only as the result of a very difficult job, as is so often the case with new fathers, the consequences can be lasting and tragic.

One day, we are living lives that we can trace with some thread of consistency. The next day, everything has changed so much we are mystified at how it happened. Somehow, the boundaries of our existence have expanded dramatically. We can feel the enormity of the transformation, but we have no reference for understanding it or anyone to talk to about it.

Indeed, for most us, the transition to fatherhood is like being dunked into a bath of ice water: one moment, we are young men concerned largely with our wives, our careers, and our leisure time; the next moment, we are fathers—not at all sure about what we are supposed to do, but with a very definite sense that the scope of our responsibility has just increased enormously.

The urge to provide and protect is very powerful, but don't let it force you into a one-dimensional role.

Build a powerful sense of connection

One of life's greatest mysteries is reconciling our existence as unique individuals with the reality that we are intricately connected to everyone and everything. We are, in fact, both alone and connected.

As men, we are intimately familiar with the first truth. Very early in life, we learn that we are on our own. We are schooled in isolation; we learn to accept it as a natural part of our existence, and we create a safe place inside ourselves to which we can retreat. From this place we can, if necessary, dismiss anything outside ourselves as unimportant. This ability of men to become islands unto themselves is also what allows us to pursue our dreams, interests, and goals with dogged determination. We can strip away everything else and bear down on precisely what we want.

This capacity to retreat to a place of our most basic needs is a powerful survival mechanism, and, as ruthless as it appears, it is very effective. Cross us, attack us, insult us, hurt us, and we can survive by retreating to this place, where nothing that the other person says or does is important. Unfortunately, although this skill can be very useful on the battlefield, it can be very destructive when employed with those we hold most dear.

The second part of the paradox of aloneness and connection is what has always caused us trouble. For we are very good at retreating to our island, but we are not nearly so skilled at extending ourselves to others, building a bridge to someone else. It is an undertaking that requires great faith and courage, because the very act of acknowledging our connection forces us to drop our defenses and makes us vulnerable.

The currency of that connection is love and, for most men, our love for our children is the safest and most stable place to begin. It is love that gives us the courage and audacity to extend our hands to another. It is love that grants us the courage to open the door to our inner selves and stand there, vulnerable and exposed in front of others.

It is in this space that we create the circuitry that bridges the gap between us. Here, we are able to share, at the deepest level, the most important aspects of who we are. And it is in this connection that we are able to receive the miracle of our children's love.

Very few things that we, as men, will ever experience are as deep and powerful as our love for our children. It is an extraordinarily primal, almost visceral feeling, and we don't always know how to react to it. For most of us, it is impossible to describe—we simply cannot find the words. Partly because of that, we resist talking about it. It resides inside us in a protected place, like a precious treasure that must be guarded.

Ironically, because we don't talk about it, the feeling itself becomes more powerful and mysterious, making us even more unwilling to discuss it. We're afraid that, if we try to talk about our love for our children, we will either stumble around, unable to find the proper words to convey the feeling, or, worse, that the sheer depth and power of the feeling will cause our voices to falter. Indeed, in many of the interviews I did for this book, voices cracked with emotion when fathers spoke about their love for their children.

Because it can be so overwhelming, too many of us assume that the mere existence of such a powerful feeling is sufficient for our children's well-being—but it isn't. That feeling, that unconditional love and commitment to our children, is the foundation of our future and the salvation of our past; but it is nothing unless and until we can bring it forth and offer it to our children in ways in which they can receive it.

We are all alone and we are all connected, but it is the feeling of being alone that will remain with us until we learn how to fashion the lasting bonds that connect us. We cannot experience the richness of being a part of something larger than ourselves, nor can we offer our children the security of truly feeling that they are not alone, without first being willing to take the risks entailed in learning to embrace and articulate our emotions.

This challenge cannot be avoided if we want to take our fathering seriously. For it is here, in the charged atmosphere of shared feelings, that we will truly meet our children. It is here, in the articulation of our deepest feelings, that we can weave the deep chords of strength that will sustain our children throughout their lives. And it is here, face to face with the unconditional love of our children, that we will receive the greatest of gifts.

2

Dad Is Different and Can Make a Difference!

Living life to the fullest requires taking risks. On one level, this is completely obvious: just identifying a need raises the distinct possibility that we won't be able to satisfy it. Ask a favor and risk being turned down. Ask for a date and risk rejection. Start a new business and risk financial ruin. Everything, from the most inconsequential to the most important things in life, requires us to put ourselves, our money, our egos, our hearts, and our physical well-being at risk. Yet we live in a society that has become so focused on avoiding risks that it can be easy to forget how important it is to help our children develop the skill and courage to take them.

Teach risk-taking

Sometimes it scares me how obsessed we have become with "security." I'm terrified that my children will be too afraid to do the things they need to do to be happy and successful in their lives. I've tried, largely by example, to let them see that you just can't compromise, you can't play it safe when it comes to what you really want and believe.

Traditionally, in almost every culture, the role of teaching risk-taking behavior has fallen to fathers. From the earliest memories of our species, we have had to be prepared to risk everything to protect our children. Fathers taught children how to make their way in the wild, how to recognize dangers without letting those dangers hinder them from accomplishing their tasks. So it is today as well. The specific dangers may have changed from wild animals and enemy tribes to bullies and busy streets, but the most debilitating danger remains the same: pervasive, overwhelming, self-defeating fear. It is our job to teach our children to be fearless.

We need to expand their worlds. Some parents are so worried about protecting their children that they end up with children who are seriously handicapped. Inadvertently, we accomplish what the ancient Chinese did purposefully in the practice of binding girls' feet—we wrap them in such tight protection that they end up hobbling through life, afraid to take any risks whatsoever.

The process of learning—growing and stretching the bounds of who we are—has a built-in positive feedback loop. With each new discovery, each lesson learned, we become larger and more complete than we were before, and we gain confidence that we can continue to grow and learn. The process itself is like a self-esteem escalator, moving higher and faster all the time. The more we can do, the better we feel about ourselves; the better we feel, the more we can do.

One of the best ways to teach our children how to evaluate new situations, to understand how much risk is reasonable, and to be comfortable and unintimidated, even in completely foreign territory, is to give them a guided tour. Expose your children to the real world. Have them sort through their clothes and toys and go with you to deliver them to a local charity. Take them with you to work or on business trips.

Involve them with money. Two findings repeatedly surface from study after study: how to deal with money is one of the biggest issues of anxiety and contention among couples; and children who grow up in families that expose them to economic issues turn out to be the best managers of businesses. This is not surprising; what is surprising is how many parents continue to keep their children almost completely ignorant of real economic issues. Give your younger children an allowance for chores done around the house and yard; then make a special shopping trip so they can spend the money as they choose. Involve older kids in family financing; have them participate in planning a family vacation, complete with weighing different options that have to fit into an overall vacation budget. Let teenagers help balance the checkbook and see what groceries, gas, and insurance cost; talk to them about credit cards and about saving for college. If you own a business, expose them to the financial side as well as utilizing their labor.

When our children get themselves in over their heads, we are almost always tempted to dive in and come to the rescue. But in so doing, we rob them of the opportunity to grow that the moment of crisis presents. One of the least-discussed secrets of life is that it is precisely in such moments—when we are forced to face the very thing that appears to be the most difficult to face—that true growth and transformation can take place.

Rescuing our children prematurely can cripple them just as surely as neglect or overprotection. We need to provide them the opportunity—the benediction—to learn how to solve their own problems. In the long run, this gift will be the most valuable skill we can teach them.

This is such a difficult assignment: to stand there, knowing that you could step in and alleviate the immediate pain, yet also knowing that, by doing so, you would do more damage than good. It is a delicate balance that we must always consciously maintain. Good fathering does not stem purely out of instinct, simply because we love our children. We need to apply all our love, all our strength, and all our analytical skills in this endeavor.

Our mistakes are frequently our best teachers. They give us the hard-to-dismiss feedback we need to do better next time. Helping our children become comfortable making mistakes is an important and surprisingly difficult task. From the earliest moments of their lives, our children are constantly undertaking what seems to them to be a vast mountain range of challenges. From gaining basic control over their physical movements to speaking, reading, writing, and thinking systematically, it feels to them as if they are constantly struggling with things that everyone else (adults) can do easily and perfectly.

Teach them to set goals

As dads, we live by the goals we set, but for children, life has a way of just rolling forward like one of those moving sidewalks at the airport. Time passes, events come and go. With the exception of birthdays and graduating to the next class level, there are very few road signs announcing your accomplishments. "Congratulations, you just mastered the alphabet, or read your first adult book, or learned how to multiply, or learned your first song on the piano!"

Part of the problem is that, from our children's perspective, from the moment they are born, they are running at full tilt trying to learn all the things that it appears to them adults have effortlessly mastered. They are so focused on all the things they don't know and can't do, they hardly have time left to stop and appreciate what incredible accomplishing machines they have become. Yet, helping our children to see the extraordinary string of achievements they have under their belts is a great way to get them to see just how capable they really are.

For the most part, they aren't going to set goals for themselves and then check back in to evaluate how they did—they are entirely too swept up in the headlong rush to grow up. But that doesn't mean we can't help out. And we have a secret advantage—we know how incredible they are and what amazing things they can accomplish. So, whenever appropriate, with small things—like learning to tie their shoes, or making a cheese omelet, or homework, or school projects, or sports—help your child to set reasonable goals and then be sure to acknowledge and celebrate their accomplishments. Children who have goals and realistic aspirations, along with a plan for achieving those goals, are children who have a good sense of their accomplishments; children who feel capable have high self-esteem.

Learning experts have identified three zones that define us as learning beings. The first is the comfort zone. Here, we do what we already know how to do. Life is easy here, but there's no learning going on at all. It's a comfortable, but lazy, place. Second is the stretch zone. Here, we try new things. There's a bit of fear attached, but generally we know we are capable of doing them. We're challenged, but not overly threatened. The third is the danger zone. Here, we're overstretched, over our heads. All we experience here is panic and fear that we can't measure up.

Ask your child what one thing he or she would like to accomplish. Then help them break it down into increments and create a timeline. If the task is to dress without help, for instance, break it down into putting on socks, pants, shirt, shoes with help, shoes without help. Then create a chart with each category and mark off with a check, sticker, or star when each task is mastered. When the whole task is complete, don't forget a celebration!

Play with your children

Play is important because it is practice, but practice for what? Thanks to the wonderful people who stand behind one-way mirrors with clipboards and watch children at play, we know that, in general, girls' play tends to be about "being," while boys' play tends to be about "doing." Girls practice being caretakers with their dolls, tea sets, houses, and role-playing games, while boys fly off into competitive sports, wildly imaginative alien worlds that must be conquered, and building massive structures out of blocks.

Both forms of play are important, but the balance in our culture is way out of kilter. Practicing how to get along with others is something boys should do considerably more often, and practicing conquering the world is something girls should be doing considerably more often.

The overall picture is too muddy at the moment for us to understand fully just how much of our children's play is biologically motivated and how much is environmentally induced. What is clear, however, is that the combined force of the advertising industry and our own deeply ingrained cultural bias plays a major role in directing our children's play. When most commercials and children's programming show girls dressing up, playing house, and engaging in relatively passive games, while boys are shown kicking balls, driving toy race cars, and banging around with toy tools, the message is pretty compelling. To grow up confident in their abilities to take on the whole range of situations they will encounter, our children need to start practicing, and that means playing.

Plan for quiet time and dream time

One of the prevailing myths about boys, and particularly adolescents, is that they spend too much time alone. They disappear behind a closed bedroom door and don't appear for hours, and then only to wolf down food and return to their inner sanctum. But don't confuse private time with quiet time. Both are necessary, but quiet time is much harder to come by. For the most part, when our boys are holed up in their rooms, they are fully occupied, listening to music, banging away on the computer, talking to friends on the phone, reading, building something, drawing, or whatever. Getting them to understand the importance of real quiet time can itself be a challenge, but one that is well worth the time.

Real quiet time requires being in a place with distractions minimized. By cutting out as much external input as possible, the deeper part of ourselves can emerge. The yearnings of our hearts become more clear, our thoughts and feelings (after an initial period of racing around at light speed, confused by all the silence) begin to slow down and can be seen more clearly.

Structured retreats can be very beneficial. I used to take my son wilderness camping. We spent a few hours each day off on our own just basking quietly in the embrace of nature. Organizations like Outward Bound provide a great mixture of team-building and quiet time. Real quiet time is difficult to organize around the house because of all the existing distractions, but even that can be done if planned properly

One of the most unsettling concepts in our culture is completely unstructured time. Most of us feel the need to fill all our time, even playtime, with planned activities, leaving no gaps to "do nothing." Many of us are so busy with work and family obligations that the notion of "free time" is laughable.

There is much to be said for good planning and efficient time-management, but everyone needs to fit large chunks of unstructured time into their lives. This is particularly true for our children, who need time to dream, to "space out," to imagine their futures. "Doing nothing" is an extremely valuable lesson to pass on to our children, because it opens them to the exciting and wide world of their own interior landscapes of thoughts, feelings, and creativity that will solidify their appreciation of their extraordinary uniqueness.

When our time is completely structured, right down to the "recesses," the only things that can happen are contained within the plan—the barbecue will be great or a dismal failure; the trip to Waterworld will be wonderful fun, marred by too much arguing, or just downright lousy. What is missing is the unknowable—what might happen, what could arise, if nothing were planned.

By introducing our children to this wonderfully enticing "empty space," we introduce them to a portal into their own hearts and minds, where whatever they think or feel can emerge and be explored. We give them the tools of inner discovery, which ultimately will be their strongest allies.

Let freedom of expression reign

This seems obvious—ask any parent if they want their children to grow up strong and comfortable with their own beliefs, values, and opinions, and nine times out of ten you will get an unqualified "Of course." And it isn't surprising that studies consistently show that children with high self-esteem are most likely to come from families that encourage freedom of expression. What is surprising is how hard it is in practice to create the space for our children to have opinions and views different from our own. It's easy to let them have their opinions when they mirror ours, but as soon as they start espousing ideas that are anathema to us, we tend to react quickly and overly forcefully.

Healthy families are careful to foster an atmosphere where everyone's personal opinions are respected, even if those opinions are not universally shared. Children who feel free to express themselves without fear, judgment, or rejection are happier and feel better about themselves than children who feel they have to censor themselves to fit in. Children who are encouraged to say what they think, even if it differs from their parents' or teachers' views, are more confident, more socially secure, and less likely to be led down some garden path by peer pressure. So bring the First Amendment to life in your home!

Make dinner time family discussion time. Establish some rules: No mocking or shaming, no interrupting (kids need space to form their thoughts), and no judgments. Encourage the honoring of even the most difficult topics, the most challenging questions, and make sure the more quiet family members get a chance to speak as well.

Nurture their creativity

How many of us have a similar story to tell—an insensitive parent or teacher who squashed our budding creativity. One of our greatest human treasures is our imagination, our extraordinary capacity to reach into another dimension and pull out textures, concepts, sounds, shapes, designs, and stories that delight and enliven our lives. And what a tragedy it is that so many people are cut off from this gift because we foolishly and artificially separate people into a handful of "creative types," versus the rest of us.

Whatever you do, do not let your children lose access to their creative side because someone else decides they can't draw or have no talent for the piano. Creativity comes in a vast array of categories, and it is our job to help our children find places where they can tap into that well of wonder.

Whether it is through music, writing, painting, drawing, dancing, making puppets, performing, storytelling, imagination exercises, crafts, or other projects, simply being engaged in creative efforts gives our children the almost magical experience of bringing something unique into being that wasn't there before. This is the gift of creation, and our children get to experience the powerful feeling of being the creators.

Don't allow creativity to become performance. Teach your children that their creations are for their own satisfaction. Encourage them to express their creativity in whatever ways they like and expose them to as many options as possible. But make sure that the teachers of these forms do not evaluate, but only encourage and offer practical advice.

Children have wonderfully fertile imaginations and, left to their own devices, they will wander off into magically imagined areas just as easily as they will deal with the contents of the sandbox in which they are sitting. But as parents, we rarely challenge them to use their powerful imaginative capacities to help enrich their own resources for growing. If anything, we tend to put a damper on things by trying to get them to focus on the practical issues at hand.

Way too much "Stop doing this. . . . And start doing that" and way too little "Imagine yourself in this situation; what would you do?" The scenarios should range from the tiny to the expansive, from "What would you do if some boy kissed you and you didn't want to be kissed?" to "What would your priorities be if you were the President of the United States?" "How would you comfort a friend whose father had died?" to "What would the world look like if you could change one thing?" By actively creating hypothetical situations, we not only give our children a chance to explore life scenarios with minimal risk, to try out and learn about values and life strategies, but, at the same time, we support and honor their creative capacity and encourage their own trust and reliance on their imaginations.

Encourage an entrepreneurial spirit

Historically, men have taken more risks than women—and this has been true in entrepreneurial endeavors as well. While this has been changing in the past few decades (currently the fastest growing business category is women-owned businesses), still the children in our care need to be encouraged to take the risks that creating a business from scratch require.

Children as young as six to ten years old are capable of running the time-honored lemonade and cookies stand, while children in middle and high school can run babysitting cooperatives, lawn-mowing services, and dog-walking businesses—or whatever else they can come up with. Since the traditional jobs available to most teenagers are low-paying and dead-end, we should encourage our children to take their talents and use them to create their own businesses rather than working for peanuts at the local fast-food joint. Depending on the business, they will develop math skills (including costing jobs), organizing abilities, the rudiments of marketing, negotiating skills . . . the list goes on and on. Not to mention the boost to their sense of independence by earning their own money!

This is particularly important, since futurists claim that, in the future, the average worker will be a free agent, creating their own opportunities and moving from job to job. In this kind of environment, experience in starting an enterprise from scratch and seeing it through will be invaluable as they make their way through life.

Help your children see the opportunities right in front of them. Do you live in a place that gets lots of foot traffic and could support a stand of some sort? Does your child love young kids, and are there busy parents in the neighborhood who would like a Saturday drop-off babysitting service organized by a group of friends? By helping your children focus on the strengths and opportunities around them, you help them think about their own "natural resources" that will help them throughout life.

Empower them

Power is one of those words that gives us pause, because it can be misused so easily. All we need do is look around, and it is easy to see people close to us, as well as those in the public eye, who have a burning need to exercise power and control over others. Conversely, there are plenty of people who spend much of their time and energy trying to avoid exercising any power at all, simply out of fear of being held responsible for the consequences. It is a conflicted issue, but one that is crucially important to resolve if our children are to grow up in confident control of their own lives. They must learn to be comfortable and responsible in the holding and exercising of power, and the best way for them to learn these lessons is to start early.

Each of us, even the smallest children, needs to feel that we can influence and have some degree of control over our lives. This sense of empowerment, the opposite of helplessness, allows us to realize we can accomplish our goals and be successful. To help our children feel empowered, we must give them opportunities to solve their own problems; we must trust them to make decisions and sound judgments regarding their own lives.

But it is important to see that their responsibilities are appropriate for their maturity level and that they have access to the tools they need to succeed. By trusting them with responsibility, we show them that we have faith in their abilities. But it must be a real trust—you can't turn over the decision to them and then take it back if you don't like what they decide.

This is obviously a gradual process. Only you know when they are ready for each step. But remember, the more we allow our children to make the decisions that affect their lives, the better decision-makers they will become. Like anything else, it takes practice.

Avoid rescuing

We love our children so much that it is hard for us to see them suffer, if only for a little while, in confusion or doubt. As soon as we see they're having a problem, we tend to want to rush in and fix it.

This is particularly true with girls, who, unconsciously at least, we see as more vulnerable than boys. Studies have shown, for example, that mothers on beaches let their sons roam farther from them physically, while they try to keep their daughters right by their sides, even though neither child is out of eyesight. While it may be true that there are real dangers in the world, it is also true that such hypervigilance does less to make our children safe and more to disable them—sending them the message that we don't trust their abilities to take care of themselves.

I'm not suggesting that we not supervise our children or let them roam around unattended. What I am saying is that, unless they are in actual danger, we should allow them to figure out the solutions to their problems, rather than running in with the cold towel, the Kleenex, or the replacement homework. When we say to them, "I know you can figure this out," we send a strong message of our belief in their competence. When we say "Poor baby, come here and I'll make it all better," what we're saying is that they lack the ability to resolve the situation and must be saved by us.

This doesn't mean that they might not require help in figuring out how to solve the problem. But it does mean that we put the onus for the solution on their capable shoulders.

Encourage reading

For most of the history of civilization, the mark of a person's accomplishment and status was largely measured by whether or not they could read. If you can read, you have access to all the information and knowledge in the world. If you can't, you are stuck in a prison of ignorance. Although part of this is no longer true, since the roaring din of modern electronic media can serve as a gateway to some of that information, what television and the movies provide in special effects and glitter, they lack in depth and breadth. So much so that the real danger is forgetting how incredibly shallow and one-dimensional most TV shows and movies are.

A study conducted by Kansas State University, polling over 600 grade-school children, found that "children perceive poor readers as less friendly and less popular than good readers." Paul Rand, executive director of the Capable Kid Counseling Centers, told *Working Mother* magazine: "This perception may contribute to the correlation between poor academic performance and low self-esteem." Clearly, a love of books and an eagerness to read will contribute to a child's success in all aspects of life, including how they feel about themselves.

The world of books offers such variety and richness, so much more opportunity for the imagination to soar, that, to paraphrase Mark Twain, the difference between reading books and watching television is like the difference between lightning and the lightning bug. Raising our children with a love of books places a tremendous reservoir of possibilities at their fingertips. There are inspiring books that showcase different cultures, career options, and role models; books that serve as affirming mirrors to children's everyday experiences; fantasy books that spark the imagination; adventure stories that engage their dreams; history books that reveal the influence and accomplishments of role models throughout history.

From the earliest age, give your child books. There are cloth books, plastic books for the bathtub, and even chewable books for teething. Children as young as six months old will eagerly flip through little board books. Make reading a part of your daily ritual when your child is still an infant. Before bedtime or another quiet time, cuddle up in bed or on a comfortable couch and read and enjoy books together. It will become a cherished time for both of you.

Make success happen

One of the activities my daughter enjoyed most when she was little was playing "Chutes and Ladders" with me. For a long time, it drove me crazy, because this was a game of pure chance: you spun the dial, made your moves, and what happened, happened. It was therefore difficult for me to get at all engaged; just the sight of her running across the living room with the game in her hands and a huge smile on her face was enough to make me want to run. Until, that is, I finally figured out why she loved this game so much—she could beat me at least as often as I beat her!

It was a powerful lesson for me. She wanted an experience of success in a world where it is hard for young kids to experience it. Success experiences are not something that most of us incorporate in our parenting, but we should. For accomplishment breeds the belief that you are capable of more accomplishment, and success breeds an attitude that you can succeed.

That's why we need to go out of our way to create situations that will give our children that heady feeling of success. Whether it is games, sports, schoolwork, construction projects, hobbies—it doesn't matter as long as it provides opportunities for genuine success. In fact, the broader the spectrum of success we can create, the stronger their sense of accomplishment will be. Studies from early-childhood experiences to corporate settings consistently demonstrate that one of the most important criteria for success is believing you can succeed, and that the most important factor in believing you can succeed is having a track record of success. So start helping your child create that track record today.

One easy avenue to encourage this is sports. Success comes in many forms with sports, especially team sports. Your contribution, whatever it is, is important and highly valued by your teammates, coaches, and fans. Second, team sports provide a very concrete and supportive environment within which to learn how to turn mistakes and losses into something on which you can build. You get the experience of working hard toward specific goals; your practice and improvement is publicly encouraged and celebrated; and you learn how to accept setbacks without taking it personally.

Additionally, and often overlooked, is that you get to become comfortable with the strength, incredible beauty, and capacity of your wonderful body, which provides a strong layer of defense against the onslaught of negative body-image messages that besiege young children in our culture. When you have seen, felt, and experienced your body turn on a baseball and send it flying, make a quick elusive cut on the soccer field, crush a volleyball, or hit a twenty-foot jumper, the power and grace you feel helps you dismiss the idea that you are supposed to look a particular way.

Travel!

As adults, most of us love to travel and readily recognize what an incredibly expanding adventure it can be. But for many understandable reasons, when we become parents, we begin to prune our travel plans into smaller and more homogenized pieces. Yes, it is a hassle to travel with kids, and yes, the kinds of places we want to go and the kinds of places they want to go don't overlap too often. But we make a big mistake if we simply cut back our outings or keep going to the same kinds of kid-friendly theme parks year after year. What we lose is a truly extraordinary opportunity to expose our children to a whole different part of the world and a whole different way of looking at life.

Travel is a powerful mind-expanding experience in itself. But, by breaking us out of our daily routine, it presents whole new opportunities for interactions and communications with our children that would otherwise not exist. Go camping, go backpacking into the wilderness, trace the path of the early pioneers, drift down the mighty Mississippi and tell tales of the heyday of river trade, visit the early colonial villages in the Northeast and revisit American history, trace the route of the Erie Canal, try to visit countries where English isn't the first language.

Crack open the invisible boundaries of what "life" is supposed to look like, and let your children experience firsthand the vast richness of the world in which we live. It will go a long way toward making them feel confident and capable of handling themselves in whatever situation they find themselves.

Yes, it can be a hassle, but with some good advance planning, a willingness to be flexible, and an adventurous attitude, travel can be incredibly rewarding and can result in some of the more memorable moments in your child's life.

Involve your children in the planning of your trips. Giving them some say in what you see or where you go helps to invest them in the excursion. When you give them some responsibility for part of the itinerary, they not only gain experience in doing research and making decisions, they learn that you trust and care about their involvement.

Live and teach values

One of the fascinating recent findings about self-esteem is that simply praising kids—that is, just telling them over and over that they are wonderful—does not build self-esteem. Rather, researchers have found such comments have to be grounded in something real to affect self-concept: "You did a great job on the soccer field, Anna, the way you didn't get upset even though you missed the ball, but hung right in there and recovered well."

What this points to is the first characteristic of living with integrity: living from a consciously sincere and honest place, where the words we speak always deeply reflect the truths we feel. This is crucially important when dealing with children, because they have an unfailing "truthometer" for phoniness, contrivedness, or just plain lies. In other words, if we want to affect our children's self-esteem positively, we must mean what we say, we must be explicit and true in our praise, and we must praise them with sincerity, so that the praise resonates with them.

The second characteristic of integrity is living from a place of wholeness and completeness, not slicing our lives into small pieces that can be presented or withheld to impress or manipulate. In a world in which more people are consciously or unconsciously playing roles than are actually living from their own deeply embedded truths, integrity is an extraordinary, powerful, and rare thing. When we embrace our own lives, expose the depth of our beliefs to our children, and then actually live our lives consistent with those values, we present children with an intensely valuable model. When we then let them know that we expect the same from them, by encouraging and supporting them in discovering and developing strong values of their own, we give them a precious gift of immeasurable worth. Remember that presents are no substitute for presence.

It's pretty common these days to find families in which both parents work full-time and feel so guilty about their lack of time with their children that they attempt to compensate by providing the children with lots of material "stuff." It's an understandable impulse and, unfortunately, your children will help draw you down this errant pathway, since they love to get "stuff." But "stuff" is not what they need, and it sends a very damaging message—that love is interchangeable with, and therefore can be bought, sold, and traded for, "stuff." When that's the message being sent, suddenly your child's self-esteem is reduced to how much "stuff" they have and how good it is. And that is a formula that can lead only to disaster.

We live in a world that, for all appearances, values "stuff" more than anything, and it is essential that, in our attempts to transmit to our children the things we truly value, we let them know, in words and in deeds, how absolutely and completely wrong that message is. If you ever find yourself searching for the perfect purchase to make up for your busy schedule, stop yourself immediately. The time you spend shopping will be much better spent with your child. And while we're at it, don't make a habit of "shopping" with your child as a way of spending time together; the message is far too mixed, and it's too easy to slide over into the ugly quagmire of love equals "stuff."

Instead of presents, our children need our presence, our honest and complete focus: I am here with you, not thinking about the chores I haven't completed, not worrying about work, not distracted, not preoccupied, not emotionally removed—just here in this moment with you.

Teach a healthy respect for things

At the same time, be sure to teach your children a healthy respect for the things we need and use in our lives. By understanding what kinds of things are important and useful and treating them appropriately, we can inoculate our children against the insidious cultural addiction to accumulate things and cling to them as if objects were truly a substitute for human connection.

Rather than getting your child a new toy to replace a broken one, try to fix it, or make an attempt to find a new use for it. If a preschooler breaks something purposely—say rips a book or damages a toy—don't leap to repair the harm. When children realize the consequences of their actions, that they have to live with the torn book or the broken toy, they learn a lesson about value.

To discourage a preoccupation with material objects, model that attitude for your children. Reign in your own itch to consume for the sake of consumption. Treat the things you own with pride and care, teaching them respect for the things in your home that have special meaning for you, other than just simply monetary value. Because you use it only on special occasions, you show them that the bowl your grandmother gave you has meaning for you.

Avoid insincerity and backhanded compliments

Just as important as making sure that you are truly present when you interact with your child is avoiding that shadowy, "half-there" state of insincerity. The "That's nice, dear" thrown over the top of the newspaper; the "How was you your day at school?" tossed off more as habit than real interest. Children have the capacity to consume untold amounts of our time, so it is easy to slip into "pretend-response mode" when we put on the appearance of interacting with them, but in fact are not at all engaged. The problem is that, even though it is not intentional, the message being sent is that they are not deserving of our attention.

If you catch yourself slipping into this mode—and we all end up there once in a while—stop immediately and apologize. Explain that it is not a lack of interest in what the child is talking about; it is your own problem, whether exhaustion, distraction, or preoccupation with some particular issue.

Also, be very careful about giving the gifts of positive words and then carelessly tacking on backhanded compliments. These are statements that start out positively but make a quick turnaround and end up doing more damage than good: "You look good, considering all of those chocolate bars you ate yesterday," or "I'll always love you no matter what size jeans you have to cram into," or "Great catch, how'd you do that?" The last place our children need to hear backhanded compliments is from us. To reaffirm their growing sense of self-esteem, they need messages that signal complete engagement, support, and unconditional love.

It's amazing how we get stuck in habits of relating to our children, even when we know better. Usually, it's because we were treated that way ourselves as kids, and the patterns are deeply ingrained. This is where a spouse or loving friend can be helpful. Ask them to tell you if you have this problem.

Encourage them to be true to themselves

One of the most difficult tasks we face is helping our children live their lives with a strong sense of personal integrity. It's a difficult task, because, as they head into adolescence, their concept of "true self" is still only in the formative stages. Each year they grow, they are less and less willing to listen patiently to what we have to say; our replacements in terms of influence are their equally young and ever-changing group of friends.

We know that, when children have high self-esteem, they don't waste time and effort impressing others, because they already know they have value. It's implicit. But if they feel needy of the approval of others, they go to great lengths to get it. The desire to be part of a group, to fit in, is normal; the willingness to distort who you are in order to fit in, however, is a clear danger sign.

Watch for the kinds of compromises they appear willing to make, for signs that they are sacrificing parts of their true personality to fit in. In some cliques, it's not popular to be smart, and many children "dumb down" to be one of the gang. Suddenly, they may not want to play sports anymore, even though they love them, because "cool children" don't do that. Or they stop reading and start watching a lot of TV (in which they never used to be interested) so they can relate to the lunchroom conversation better.

This can be a very subtle and difficult call sometimes, particularly because it is natural for middle-school and teenage children to practice putting on different personae as a way of developing their own identities. But if you feel that somehow they are doing something just to fit in rather than from an intrinsic desire to do it, trust your instincts. Chances are you are right.

Provide a moral framework

Certainly a crucial part of raising children is helping to steer them away from socially unacceptable behavior and teaching them how to get along cooperatively with others. There is also a good deal of more specific line-drawing that goes on: it's not nice to hit people, it is rude to interrupt when someone else is talking, and so on.

Unfortunately, most of this "socialization" training is reactive and negative—our sweet little darling makes some social error and we intervene with a no, no, no! What is missing in this scenario is the moral framework that gives reason to the rules. Without that framework, the exchange is experienced by our children as chastisement. Even if they vaguely intuit that we may be right, the predominant experience is one of having been caught up short and read the riot act. This, in turn, engenders feelings of shame, guilt, failure, and even sometimes anger and resentment. We may get the message across by virtue of our authority, but the point is lost and the process does more to undermine their self-confidence and self-esteem than support it.

By taking the time to explain the reasons behind the rules in ways that are appropriate and understandable to their ages, we not only honor our children with the assumption that they are capable of understanding and acting accordingly, but we make it possible for them to see that this is not just a reprimand. Rather, we are trying to help them by giving them valuable information.

Rules and reprimands without well-articulated reasons appear arbitrary and an exercise of brute authority. The message is "I'm the boss, you're the kid; I have power, you don't." That message not only does nothing to help children understand the moral underpinning of your judgment, it also undermines their own sense of power and responsibility. Simply by taking the time to explain our reasoning, we allow them to work on the framework of their own emerging conscience, and we reinforce their confidence that they are fully capable of doing so.

Often we say "Because I said so" because we don't know what else to say. It helps to think about these things in advance of the moment. Why shouldn't we interrupt someone? Why is fourteen hours of TV-watching not acceptable? If we work through the scenarios in our own minds first, we'll be able to give answers that make sense in the moment.

Help them to consider others

Growing up is an egocentric undertaking. In part, this is inevitable: our children need to develop a strong sense of themselves and of their own desires and interests. It certainly should not be surprising, then, that they will, at some point or another, display behavior that is not only selfish but callously insensitive to others. Ironically, however, it is the children who were always allowed to assume center stage, who always got what they wanted, and who were allowed to get away with just about anything that grow into the young adults with low self-esteem. Being deferred to, catered to, and coddled may satisfy some self-centered childish need, but it leaves a child without the experience, resources, or confidence to function outside that distorted cocoon.

Conversely, children who are taught from early on that they are not the center of the universe, and that we all have a responsibility to be concerned about the people and world we live in, tend to have much higher self-esteem. This is not only because their childhood experiences of learning the limits, rules, and responsibilities more accurately reflect the experiences they will be faced with as adults, but because the very concept of being responsible for people and things outside of oneself is empowering. It is, in itself, a statement that you are needed, that your energy and your efforts are important to others and to the world at large. Indeed, a healthy sense of social responsibility can be one of the most powerful components in building a healthy, self-confident personality, because it confers a purpose that is larger than yourself.

Everyone wants to be of use. Help your children figure out how their unique talents can be of use in the world, right now, not just when they're grown. Is your daughter wonderful with animals? Perhaps she can volunteer at a wild animal rescue foundation. Is your son a great swimmer? Maybe he can teach swimming to disabled kids. Give them the chance to contribute.

3

Focus on the Big Issues!

For quite some time now, any serious discussion of gender has been studiously avoided simply because it feels like a minefield that elicits heated emotional responses rather than curious and probing exploration. Yes, we have had the surface-skating, back patting, let's-laugh-at-ourselves self-help books like *Men Are from Mars and Women Are from Venus*, but when the president of Harvard University can be fired just for asking the question whether gender may have something to do with the huge academic-achievement gap between women and men in science and math, you know that any real exploration of the issue is fraught with danger. Unfortunately, the greater danger now is not talking about the issue.

Talk about a new model of masculinity

It is no secret that the last fifty years have witnessed a veritable revolution in how we see and what we expect from men and women. Until now, most of that change has been initiated by, and largely about, women. Someday, we will look back on this time as an astonishingly rapid refashioning of the definition of what a woman is. And while it is certainly not a completed process, compared to the confusion surrounding male identity, it paints a strikingly clear picture.

The same cannot be said of what it means to be a man, which is very much something that has yet to emerge. We can provide for and protect our children, and support them in their efforts to grow happy and healthy; we encourage them to follow their dreams, hone their emotional intelligence, and live connected to their hearts. But, at the same time, we need to give them at least some idea of what it means to be a man.

It's a mark of how blinded we are as a culture that one of the core questions with which our children have to struggle is not even an acceptable topic of conversation. What is clear is that our definition of a good man is in a tumultuous and confusing transition. The old models, from knights in shining armor to John Wayne, still hold some attraction, but are clearly one-dimensional and inadequate. The new models that appear out of the "Sensitive New Age Guy" sitcom portrayal of fumbling manhood offer half-baked alternatives riddled with their own inadequacies.

As fathers, we are smack in the middle of this extraordinary transformation, even if we are not always sure exactly where it is heading. So our first obligation is to be as clear as we can with our children about the changing nature of masculinity itself, and that includes the humility to admit we don't know all the answers. Ultimately, a new definition of manhood will emerge from the minds and hearts of our children and grandchildren as they grow and develop. The largest responsibility for the creation of a new definition of manhood is theirs to discover, to experience, to experiment with, and to refine. What we can do is provide them with the context to understand this awkward time and open the discussion. We can support them in their efforts, and create a strong support system around them that reinforces the benefits of emotional expression and deep interpersonal connection.

So how do we help our children make sense of this? How can they possibly know what direction they need to go? By talking about it. By shining the bright light of reason, or at least the warm light of compassion, on this murky and frightening issue. We may not have the answers yet; we may not be able to articulate exactly how a man should be strong without being violent or angry, sensitive and compassionate without losing self-focus and determination, generous without giving himself away. We may not have a clear picture of how we want the pieces to fit together, but if there is a better topic of ongoing conversation, I can't think of it.

Let your children know that they are an important part of an extraordinary process of redefining what it is to be a man and regularly invite their active participation in exploring what that definition should be.

Get them comfortable with change

Edmund Burke gave us a great quote that you have undoubtedly heard many times: "Those who don't know history are destined to repeat it." Perhaps we need to add that, to live consciously in this rapidly changing world, it is also true that those who do not understand where they are in the context of change have little chance of responding appropriately.

We all know that things seem to be changing a lot faster than ever before, but we need to face a deeper truth that our children's lives will, to some degree, be measured by how well they can adapt to change. While this may seem obvious, it is worth taking time to focus on, because, in fact, this is a radical departure from the way humans have lived since they emerged from the African savannah. We used to learn all the information and skills we needed at our parents' knee and then pass it along to our children. This cycle has been going on for generations. Things just did not change all that much from one generation to the next.

In today's world, however, everything is changing—technology, climate, work and living environments, and, much more significantly, social relationships, including gender roles. By focusing on helping our children understand the changes that are taking place in our gender roles, we can perhaps also give them the observational and intellectual tools to understand more clearly their place within the other changes taking place all around them.

We are, after all, a product of our history, and that is truer in how we perceive our roles as men and women than we may care to admit. Gender roles have been handed down from generation to generation. Often, these roles were rooted in very practical and useful historical divisions of labor and only became constricting later, when the circumstances that gave rise to them changed, but the role separations continued.

One of the most enjoyable ways to explore this history and unravel what made sense then that no longer makes sense now is to go back in time with your children and explore the world of gender roles. Expose them to stories of other cultures in which things were divided up differently. Give your children the gift of perspective and the challenge of imagination. Use history to open their minds to what the present is and what the future should be. Through history books, historical fiction, historical movies, and active imagination, try to capture with your sons what life must have been like in prehistoric times, when people lived in small tribes, at the dawn of agriculture, during the rise of the first great civilizations on Earth. Talk about life expectancies, the dangers and challenges of each period, and wonder with your children about why men and women assumed different roles at different times. Have your children imagine what they would have felt like living at different times, what they would have dreamed of doing. Then bring them closer and closer to our time and examine how the roles have changed; imagine what the future may hold and what changes they think should happen.

Be explicit about social expectations

If we are going to help our children create their own future, we first have to help them identify the culturally embedded expectations that litter the landscape of a growing child's life. The best way to deal with things that hide in the shadows is to drag them out into the light and pick them apart until we understand the how and why of their existence. Be strong, get good grades, go to a good university, graduate in the top of your class, get a good job, get married, have kids. How often is this mantra, or a variation on it, repeated in a child's life, and yet how often do we stop to ask why? When we fail to address this crucial question, we leave our advice out there as an end in itself, as if it itself were the path to salvation.

Remember how much we used to hate it when someone answered our question "Why?" with the words "because I said so!"

And what about the implicit expectations children pick up watching television and from their peers? Girls are supposed to be skinny, cute, and not terribly aggressive; boys are supposed to be—what? OK, maybe we really don't know what boys are supposed to be, but you know there will be pressures out there to which your children are responding.

Expectations, whether socially induced or our own personal expectations (as in "When you grow up, you can be a lawyer like your dad"), certainly allow for possible paths, but they can weigh very heavily on a child's shoulders. How many people do you know who did what was expected of them and are now stuck in miserable situations? If we are to prepare our children to follow their own unique paths, we first need to dismantle all the blocks that have caused them to believe that they should live by what others expect of them.

Ask your children what they think is expected of them in life. Then articulate your own expectations, but make sure to give them reasons, not just a laundry list. That way, you give them the tools they need to find their own paths and not just your idea of what that path should be.

Help them find their passion

Our job in life is to find the thing about which we are passionate and bring it into the center of our lives. That is difficult enough under the best of circumstances, but can be near impossible when the very resources we need to discover—and tap—our passions are systematically denied to us. As parents, we all want our children to lead happy, fulfilling lives. Yes, we want them to be successful and comfortable, but not at the expense of their happiness. Yet that goal can never be reached unless and until they discover the deepest parts of themselves, where their passion and purpose reside. As parents, we can help, both by encouraging and supporting them in their exploration of their emotional and spiritual selves, and by paying close attention to the things that excite them.

Children often move through phases of interest, trying out one thing or another and then suddenly losing interest. Don't let this pattern lull you into complacency. Get engaged in each and every interest they develop. Help them explore it, support their interest, encourage their experimentation, kindle their enthusiasm. But be careful not to appropriate it yourself or assume that a child who loves photography today is going to be a photographer. That kind of pressure can cause kids to withdraw altogether. Ask your children today what most excites them, and engage in a conversation about it.

Study after study has found that the single most important characteristic of people who feel happy and fulfilled in their lives is that they are engaged in doing something about which they are passionate. Conversely, one of the hallmarks of seriously depressed people is a lack of strong interest in anything. Ironically, the incredible technological changes of the past fifty years may well be making it more difficult for children to experience that kind of deep engagement. Not only has the variety of "things" we can do expanded astronomically, tempting us to dabble in everything and never become really absorbed in one thing, but the culture itself has veered radically toward prepackaged entertainment; growing up is becoming more and more a spectator sport.

Help your child discover what captures their interest: a new hobby, pursuing a special interest, starting a collection, practicing to become the softball queen. What the hobby or collection is isn't that important; it's the thrill of diving into something new that is all theirs. They can revel in the delight of learning all about it, practicing it, and mastering it—crucial steps that everyone needs to learn in order to succeed in life. In collecting coins, earrings, bugs, dolls, anything really, a child gets a lot of gratification hunting for things, sorting and studying, storing, and owning them. They have the satisfaction of realizing they have an interest that is all their own, not one that they have to share with anybody. They learn important lessons of autonomy and self-determination, proving that they are developing uniquely.

And don't get disappointed when the stamp collection goes in the closet never to come out again. It's common for children to have major mood swings, change their minds frequently, have revolving interests, and new friends. That is just part of tasting life and trying out different ideas, attitudes, and roles. The frenetic energy that many children have in preadolescence and the teen years is all a very healthy part of finding their place in the world and forging an identity, even if it can drive adults to utter frustration. Just remember, we're the ones having trouble dealing with all this quick-change artistry. For them, it's a fun and exciting time (with a lot of angst thrown in to boot). So try to relax, open yourself to and involve yourself in your child's whirlwind of a world, and you'll both be better off.

Help them sort through their ideas and experiences by actively listening and by remaining scrupulously nonjudgmental. Support their enthusiasm for new interests; engage them in lively conversations that help them think through their ideas.

Build rituals of connection

In "the old days," family, clan, tribal, or village rituals were a central part of growing up. Indeed, it was through these traditions that children became meaningfully rooted as a part of the group and learned their place within it. They were a way to teach the importance of continuity and connection, to initiate children into the deeper fabric of life, and to provide a strong experience of identity. In modern culture, the world of ritual has been stripped down to a handful of national or religious holidays whose meaning has all too often been diluted by commercialization. And now, with the intrusion of technology into our fast-paced world, even getting together regularly for dinner is challenging.

Frequently, parents of young children are in the most hectic phase of their own lives. Preoccupied with nurturing their marriage, keeping in touch with friends, taking care of all the material issues of house and home and family, and investing time building a career identity, it's easy to let the kids head off on their own, and even to be relieved when they do.

One way to counteract this is to reestablish the good old-fashioned tradition of eating together. It's amazing how many of us have almost completely given up on family dinners. Despite the obstacles (differing schedules and taste buds), it is, however, still well worth the effort, even if you have to compromise on the number of family dinner nights per week. Remember, you don't want this to be punishment; it should be a collective opportunity to reconnect in a judgment-free environment.

If you don't already, plan for at least one family meal a week, attendance mandatory. Expand the opportunity for connection by rotating cooking and cooking-assistant positions throughout the family. Then, when you sit down, focus on the positive; don't use this precious time to complain, criticize, or hand out advice.

We also need to create as many regular opportunities to get away from the normal flow of day-to-day life and move instead into sacred time together, time where the purpose is to honor and celebrate the deeper connection between us. Create your own traditions, and don't let anything get in their way.

Make the traditions you observe meaningful by seeing holidays as more than excuses to buy presents or go to the amusement park. Reinject them with the meaning they are supposed to carry. Invent new traditions, and not always traditions that include everyone. Make them special traditions between you and one of your children, be it a regular breakfast, a monthly walk in the woods, semiannual wilderness camping trips, an evening out together each month—whatever feels right for you and your child. Stick with the tradition and imbue it with that special quality of time set apart.

Articulate your values

If we want our children to live lives full of purpose and meaning, the very best thing we can do is to live our own lives as an
example. In our fast-paced, harried world, the temptation is always there to cut corners, to get to the point, to get to the result,
to cross things off our lists as quickly as possible and move on to
the next task. In the process, we become sleepwalkers, moving
through our lives without life moving through us.

What is our purpose? What values guide us through the
course of our own lives? The more we examine these things for
ourselves, and the more we discuss them with our children, the
more we offer them a worthwhile model for living. If we want
more for our children than a life on the corporate treadmill, we
need to articulate and demonstrate how to navigate using our
own personal values.

The truth is, at some level, we are all living our values;
we just haven't examined them. But our choices reveal what's
important to us: earning a six-figure salary; having a beautiful
home; making a difference; creating a close family. We each have
some core value.

We spend incredible amounts of time and energy preparing
our children to be successful and accomplished. We send them
to the best schools, help them with their homework, worry
with them over emotional issues. But far too often, we neglect the very foundation of their lives—their spiritual selves.
Life is so much more than successfully handling the material
and emotional issues that arise. Life has meaning and purpose;
each of us exists uniquely within the greater web of life to find
and walk our own path in connection with and support of the
greater whole.

To prepare our children for this role, we need to share with them our own deepest feelings and beliefs. We need to open the doors to this extraordinary world of depth and beauty so that they can begin to get their bearings, to see their part in the grand design, and to take comfort in the connection to something so much greater than their individual lives.

Take some time to think about your values and talk about them with your family.

Teach independence and respect

Independence is traditionally a big issue for boys (Be your own man; don't be tied to any apron strings; keep your own counsel; and don't let anyone in too close or you may lose your independence). This is increasingly true for girls as well. The theme has deep roots in this country, and it has tragic consequences. For the kind of "independence" into which boys are usually pushed is not independence at all, but isolation and disconnection. Ultimately, it leads to a life that is nothing but a shallow illusion.

Although this model is celebrated in a constant stream of the "strong-silent-type" heroes of movies and stories, it is in fact the most pathetic place any human being could ever find himself—cut off from any real meaning, disconnected from any real feeling, apart from any true community. These people can become so independent that, for all practical purposes, they don't exist in the stream of life other than as self-focused actors.

Real independence means having the strength, understanding, and wisdom to live your life deeply, fully, and with integrity, regardless of what others think. It means having the courage to expose yourself to risk, to navigate the deep waters of life that can only be experienced in connection to others. It means to live continually and fearlessly from your heart, from where you can experience the incredible richness of life. It means recognizing, celebrating, and holding on to your uniqueness, while at the same time sharing it as completely and constantly as possible with others.

Celebrate Independence Day by reminding your children that real independence is not about isolation and control. It is about living life with as much honesty, integrity, and depth as you possibly can.

When we think of respect, we usually associate it with people of great accomplishment, but that is not respect. We may admire what they have accomplished and believe that they handle themselves well, but real respect goes much deeper and should be dispensed universally. Life is infinitely complex, and every one of us has had to walk our own path. At any point in that journey, we may falter, we may make mistakes large and small, we may seem unkind or unappreciative, but how and why we have reached that point is our own problem. We each pay the price for our own mistakes.

Real respect encompasses the deep compassion we should hold for every person, regardless of their circumstances. It is an important lesson to pass on to our children, because, in the competitive world, it is far too easy to fall into angry, judgmental behavior and to treat other people disrespectfully. Help your children understand that those who may "disrespect" them are worthy of their compassion too, for they are so insecure that they can't do anything else.

Talk about sex

We all know we're supposed to talk about sex with our children. But just in case you need it, there is another important reason to talk to your children about sex that is not usually discussed: it helps them understand that strong feelings are not supposed to be hidden in a closet somewhere.

Sex is powerful and, of course, that is one of the reasons we feel so awkward talking about it. But get over it. When children go through puberty, sexual desire, particularly in our highly sexualized culture, can rise to surging peaks that feel, at times, almost overwhelming. The important word here is "feel." It is a distinctly physical sensation, but it is so much more. When, as parents, we tiptoe around the subject of sex, pretending it doesn't exist, we not only fail our children in their need to understand this powerful gift, we reinforce the age-old message that anything associated with "feeling" is not to be discussed!

And we are delivering this message at a time when our children most need our help. The results are often a general emotional shutdown. How many parents have you heard complaining that their sweet darling child went through puberty and turned into a silent sullen creature? One of the long-term dangers of abandoning our children to a silent sexual emergence is that sex and emotions can get tied up together in a confused, distorted, and shame-filled package that can result in sex being the only avenue to the emotions at all.

Yes, this is difficult territory, but crucially important. We need to raise our children to feel comfortable talking about sex in an emotionally shame-free environment if we want them to grow up to be able to access and manage and rely on their own emotional maturity. Start talking about sex long before it becomes necessary; it makes it easier both for you and for them. Sometimes, adolescents talk more easily about sex with knowledgeable adults who are not their parents. If you can't play this role, find someone who can.

Help them deal with fear

Fear is a powerful and, unless faced head on, a very debilitating emotion. Yet the message our children continue to get is badly distorted by old gender stereotypes. Our boys grow up convinced that they are supposed to be fearless. In the language of small boys, to be fearless is to be a man, and that is a burden they should never have to carry. And our daughters often still get the message that they should be fearful of entirely too many things.

Think about how boys are always challenging each other, daring each other to do stupid or even dangerous things—rock fights, jumping off buildings, climbing tall trees, drag racing. Likewise girls are all too often taught to squeal at the sight of frogs and lizards. A good part of the culture of boys is centered around determining who is tough and who is chicken, and the message is bluntly simple: if you are afraid, you aren't one of us. The peer pressure among girls is often the exact opposite.

But fear is a very useful survival mechanism, and we need to help our children learn that it is a normal, even appropriate, emotion that can literally save their lives. We also need to teach them how to identify the real source of their fear when it arises and how to decide upon the proper response. This isn't easy territory, because sometimes the proper response is to get yourself out of the situation as fast as possible, and sometimes it is finding a way to control your fear in order to do the right thing.

But unless we address the issue in a very supportive and open manner, we will leave them to the not-so-tender instruction of their peers.

Let your children know that we are all afraid at times, and often for very good reasons. But more important, help them learn how to understand and properly respond to their fears, and never shame them for being afraid.

Explore your own assumptions

Living at a time of great transformation is exciting, especially when the changes taking place are long overdue and coming at a dizzying pace. But it is also extremely challenging, because, as pioneers of change, we are constantly entering new territory in which we have only a general idea of what direction to take. It takes enormous energy and focus to sort out the paths and figure out what we need to do to make this journey easier for our children. Most of us are more than willing to commit this energy and time, because we want to provide our children with full and rich lives that will serve as a solid foundation for their growth and development into the extraordinary men and women we know they can be.

By far the most difficult part of our task is discovering and dismantling the places where our own training hinders our role as pioneers. Someone must go first, and it is both a great honor and a solemn responsibility. But we need to remember that our own training and our own complex array of assumptions were forged in different times, under different circumstances. Many are no longer appropriate for or supportive of our immediate task. Simply replaying past expectations, assumptions, and traditions will not change the landscape one iota. We, as a society, are in very challenging times that demand our most rigorous attention. At the same time, there is much value in the traditions of our past, and it would be foolish to jettison the whole without first thinking and feeling deeply about the ways we need to modify our own assumptions.

How many times, when talking to your children, have you heard words coming out of your mouth and been struck by the thought that these are not really your words at all, but a replay of words you heard from your parents, words they probably heard from their parents, and so on down the generations?

Gender roles are the most obvious place to start. The past forty years have seen a tremendous shift in how we view gender roles, thanks largely to the millions of women who have demanded fuller and more equal participation in life. But don't fool yourself into thinking we have turned the corner. Cultural patterns of thousands of years aren't changed in a few decades; we are in the position of the battleship just turned at the helm but that will take another twenty miles before actually making the adjustment in course.

In addition, the advances made by women have not been matched by men. Where women's lives have blossomed with opportunities, men are, for the most part, still stuck in the old ways.

Real men know how to be fathers

Encouraging boys to remain connected to their emotions and showing our daughters that men can have intelligent conversations about their feelings require the full and active engagement of their fathers. Yet too many fathers let this, one of the most valuable contributions they can make to their children's development, slip away. Sometimes, the hesitation arises out of awkwardness and inexperience. We weren't raised to be nurturing parents, we weren't given even the basic information about caring for infants and toddlers, so the easy way is simply to back away and leave it to their mom.

Sometimes, the hesitation comes from outside pressure, social expectations, and, particularly, pressure from the workplace that gives the message: "If you want to get ahead, you must put your job ahead of your children." But what father would actually endorse that message? Being a father today requires a very different kind of courage—the kind that anchors us to our deeper priorities, gives us the strength and commitment to pioneer for our children a new and more fully integrated way of living. It means being mindful of the pressures that pull us away from our children. It means stepping firmly into the whirlwind of emotions that define growing up. It means adding your voice to the rising swell of women's voices demanding flexible work hours and corporate support rather than resistance to employees with families.

Fathers need to demonstrate through their words and actions that their children's emotional needs are just as high a priority as providing food and shelter. Reassess your work schedule and make sure it allows you to be with your children when they need you. Reassess the level and quality of your involvement at home and make sure that you are doing your share.

4

Be There!

Fathering is different from mothering. We come to our task from the outside and, captured in that configuration is the miracle we have to offer. For true fathering is not the physical act of planting a seed; it is the conscious decision to tend and nourish the seedling. Real fathering is not biological—it is the conscious choice to build an unconditional and unbreakable emotional connection to another human being.

Consciously choose to be a father

Once we make that choice, it cannot be unmade. We can't abandon our children no matter what the circumstances. We can't simply turn them over to someone else for safekeeping, not even if an ex-wife is doing everything in her power to make a continued connection impossible. We can't wander off for a couple of years to get our lives together or in search of adventure. We can't turn our backs on them if they get into trouble.

The miracle of fathering, the extraordinary power it possesses to comfort, to heal, and to transform, is the manifest proof that, as a people, we are not as self-centered, not as alone, not as alienated as we sometimes fear. It proves that we can be responsible for one another, that we can eagerly embrace the often difficult task of fathering this tiny unknown mystery, and finally, that we can and will dedicate ourselves to caring for one another. In that choice, we return full circle to a life of deep connection.

In one very important sense, our own process of growing up has been a process of disconnection—the gradual disentangling from our parents, the slow but inevitable untying of the threads that forcibly hold us to them. We are "grown up" when we successfully disconnect—when we assume full control of and responsibility for our own lives. In a very powerful sense, when we first step out of the shelter of our parents' lives, we enter a kind of timeless waiting room, where the past is simply a backdrop and the future seems a promise of endless possibilities.

Perhaps what is most frightening at this juncture in our lives—when we are just beginning to exercise the skills necessary to control our own destiny—is that our options seem virtually limitless. We can dive into a traditional career path or retreat into a life of solitude and contemplation. We can experiment wildly with interests and lifestyles or delve deeply into one very specific and narrow area. We can even choose to reject the past completely and abandon any responsibility to the future. In a sense, it is the time of the full blossoming of our inherent free will.

Yet no matter how it feels, this time is but a moment in our lives. Eventually, we begin making choices that alter the landscape of life either slowly or swiftly. Deciding to become a father is one of those choices, and it defines and expands our personal universe every bit as dramatically as the primordial Big Bang defined and expanded the larger universe surrounding us.

As fathers, we become links in a chain that stretches across time, instantly and irrevocably connecting us to our ancestors and our descendants. As fathers, we also become an integral part of our community, because that is where our children will live and grow, and because it is our responsibility to do whatever we can to ensure that their community is a safe place alive with possibilities.

And as fathers, we are forced to confront the deepest spiritual meanings of life. Through the act of conception, we add our seed to the next generation and, in so doing, actively participate in renewing and perpetuating the family of man. This is not something that can be done without wondering why, without searching for meaning and a purpose, without being willing to hold ourselves open to ever-deeper and more profound insight. For the most part, however, this dramatic change takes place without our awareness, at least initially, because the process of fathering is every bit as much about our own growth and development as it is about our children's. Just as we owe a sacred bond of responsibility to our children, so must we be responsible to our own challenges—as individuals, as members of an extended family and of our local and global community, and as active participants in the wondrous mystery of life.

Understand your own family story

At times, it seems that, at the very core, human nature is an exquisite paradox—we search throughout our lifetime to discover and become who we already are. As our children begin their long search to bring to full fruition their emerging identities, they will be helped enormously by parents who have honestly and diligently mapped out the common territory. In this capacity, as mapmakers for our young explorers, the most important territory to record and pass on is that of our own family.

More than any other influence on our lives, our family will both distort and contribute to who we are. Through our genes, through the intense process of socialization, and through the deepest imprinting of psychological issues, it is our family—parents, siblings, grandparents, aunts, uncles, cousins, and extended, albeit ill-defined, others—who have the most profound effect on shaping our understanding and perceptions of all that is around and within us.

Our family is our hometown, one we pass on to our children. If we do not prepare them with as much information as we can about the side streets and back alleys, the hidden cupboards and secret stairwells, the hopes, dreams, and tragedies of this intimate place, we send them out into the world without a map or a compass.

To do this, we need first to do our part. We must face what we have been given—flaws and all—and commit ourselves to passing on the best of what our family has to offer, while trying our damnedest not to perpetuate some of the more damaging themes. That means understanding our own history, untangling the truth from the lies, and dispelling the myths and mists that obscure our vision.

Facing and accepting our roots also means honoring and appreciating the gifts we have been given—regardless of the source—and uncovering the often buried histories, hopes, and dreams of our parents and other family members. We must do this in order to give our children a place to begin, a context within which they can understand from whence they came, to see clearly the forces that have so powerfully influenced their lives.

Revisit your childhood

One of the most surprising gifts that comes from being deeply involved in the nurturing of children is the chance it offers us to revisit our own childhood emotional issues—only this time, with the consciousness and compassion of adults. As much as we may appear to children as "all grown up," we know how bruised and fragmented we really are. Our children offer us this special bonus, this rare opportunity to grow up again, only this time better than before.

As we experience and participate in the unfolding of a young child's life, our own childhood memories and experiences resurface, some pleasantly and others perhaps painfully. We have all seen this inevitable childhood return played out poorly and destructively by parents who try to live vicariously through their children, but it is just as powerfully an opportunity to heal old wounds if it is pursued with awareness.

By nurturing our children well, by doing properly the things that were never done right for us, we can heal and smooth over many of the bumps and bruises of our own child-hood. Through the love we show for our children, we can re-pair some of that damage to our own self-worth that may still linger from childhood. With self-reflection, conscious choices, and, if necessary, some good therapy, we can grow with our children and, at the same time, show them by our example that one is never too old to grow.

Be responsible for the world they will inherit

Being a father means we are responsible for our community—from the neighborhood we live in to the frightening global threat of ecological devastation. This wounded world, this troubled community of man, is the legacy we pass on to our children. Unfortunately, these already badly damaged goods are in serious danger of spiraling out of control into a hellish oblivion. If we are to honor our responsibility as fathers, if we are to hold our heads high, knowing that we have done our duty without fear, we have no choice but to do whatever we can to instill kindness and compassion into our public institutions and to fight for programs and policies that promote the healing of our community and our world.

What we have been given is the sum of our forefathers' efforts—their achievements and their failures. What we pass on to our children will bear our mark. No one man can change the direction of history, but each of us, fully embracing our responsibility as fathers, can add our voice, our shoulder, our time, and our effort. When all is said and done, if we have taught our lessons well, our children will rightfully judge us, not only by the strength and depth of our connection to them, but by the earnestness of our commitment to the world we pass on to them and our willingness to seek answers to even the most difficult questions.

Seize the deeper moments

For some mysterious reason, one of the most difficult things for men to admit is what we don't know. The larger the ignorance, the more difficult it is for us to face up to it. This may explain why we are so good at and spend so much time at the very focused and practical things and are so uncomfortable in the arena of abstract emotions and unanswerable questions. We can teach our children to throw a baseball, tune up a car, analyze a problem, get from here to there, and balance a checkbook. But ask us why we are here, what life is all about, how we know what is right, what love is, and what happens when we die—and we sputter to a halt.

These are questions about which we can only speculate, areas in which there are no answers, only beliefs. Tackling these questions can be like passing an uncomfortable frontier, but we owe it to our children to stake out our territory no matter how tenuous, no matter how difficult it is for us to explain or justify. Our children deserve to know us—to know who we are and what we believe. We may be wrong, they may disagree, but we owe them the answers in which we choose to believe. For these are the answers that give meaning and purpose to our lives.

In thinking about these larger issues, one thing emerges with striking clarity. It is moments—not days, weeks, or months, but individual, crystal-clear moments—that we remember and cherish, that become for us the symbols, the milestones, the precious content of our lives. We are connected across time, but it is only in the moment that we live. As fathers, we need to find ways to share this simple but profound truth with our children. One way to capture these precious moments is consciously to slow the frantic whirl of activity that makes up so much of our lives. Stop moving, stop talking, stop thinking. Breathe slowly and deeply, inhaling the fragrance and texture of an individual moment. Feel the sun on your face, the wind brushing through the hair on your arm, the touch of your child's hand, the smell of your newborn's cheek. It is here, in these particular moments, that we are most profoundly alive and can connect most deeply with our children.

Sometimes, like the grace we say before a meal, such rituals remind us that the small things we take for granted are actually daily miracles for which to be thankful. At other times, like the private rituals and code words we use, they remind us of the deep connection that lies just beneath the surface.

Sometimes, such personal rituals, like celebrating birthdays, bar mitzvahs, and special events, honor momentous rites of passage. At their core, their purpose is always to mark and hold on to a single moment: by bringing us together, by reweaving the powerful threads of connection, by reminding us that, as much as we are all very much alone, so too we are all bound up in this life together. The ways we choose to observe and honor our connections with our children will evolve as we grow, but we will never stop being their fathers.

Fathering is forever. The form and content evolve and transform over time, but the heart of being a father, the deep emotional bond between a father and his child, the moments when we take the time to live fully continue to exert their power well beyond our lifetime.

Lean on friends

Dads can get lost, and, like the oft-told joke, we for some reason refuse to stop and ask for directions! One of the most difficult things for fathers to do is turn to others for support. We know the reasons: our difficulty articulating and expressing emotions, our competitiveness, our pride, our raw inexperience in this arena. It is probably our greatest weakness, because it forces each one of us to reinvent fathering all over again—particularly if we are struggling with the distance created by too much travel, divorce, or just too many hours at work.

I have a friend I've known for twenty years. When we were younger, we hung around together, we both got married and had kids, and then we both got divorced. We still see each other fairly regularly. When we get together, we talk about sports and current events and sometimes work-related issues. A few months ago, we were at a baseball game, and he was brooding about something. Well, one thing led to another, and it turned out his fifteen-year-old daughter, who lives with her mother, had gotten pregnant, and he was really upset because he felt as if he had not done a good enough job keeping himself firmly in her life.

We spent the entire afternoon talking about our kids and the problems and issues we were having trying to be good fathers. It was really a wonderful experience, and later that night, I realized that I had never—and I mean never—talked about these things with anyone before. There was a part of my mind that just couldn't believe it. Here I was with two kids of my own and two stepchildren—all already well into their teens—and I hadn't talked about being a father to anyone. It's enough to make me believe men must have portions of their brains that just lock up sometimes.

I also realized, after talking to my friend, that he had let his daughter down, but it wasn't because he didn't love her and it wasn't because he didn't want to be bothered. It was because he didn't know what to do. He didn't have a clue how to make himself an important part of her life from 200 miles away.

Find a way to connect

What works for one child won't necessarily work for another, so we need to become masters of alternative forms of connection. It's up to us to adjust to our children's needs, not vice versa. The better we can tailor our approach to the individual communication styles of our children, the more we will become a vibrant force in their lives. What we need to do is anything and everything that works to pry open their hearts. And that means searching for the avenues that lead most directly into each of our children's lives.

Sometimes, we need to stretch the boundaries of imagination in order to be a constant force in our children's lives. They come in so many different configurations, and by virtue of having become fathers, it is now our responsibility—not theirs—to figure out just what is necessary to get through to them.

It is important to remember that distance between children and fathers can be measured in miles, but also in heartbeats. Both kinds of distance have consequences, but ultimately, the distance for which we cannot compensate, the kind that leaves lasting wounds, is emotional distance. It is the thunderous silence of a broken connection, the unmistakable absence of something we know should be there, the unbearable strain of waiting for a feeling that never comes. And that can happen no matter where you live.

Emotional distance can begin in the next room or the next city. And although there are extreme cases where that distance appears as a purposefully erected barrier, it is almost always an unintended and unwanted impediment. Perhaps it stems from our biological position of beginning from the "outside," but, at times, it appears as if there is a gravitational force pulling us away from a deep emotional bond with our children. If we live our lives without thinking about it, without paying close attention to what kind of fathers we want to be, the distance can seep into the cracks and expand until, one day, we find ourselves on the other side of a wide and gaping chasm.

Your real job is being Dad

For most fathers, even if we live with our children, the gravest danger pulling us away from our children is work. There are so many forces pushing us toward spending more and more time at work that we end up spending long hours away from home, bringing work back from the office, and working weekends and evenings. Many of us have jobs that take us away for days, weeks, or even, particularly for military fathers, months at a time.

The struggle to balance work and our kids is a difficult one, because, for the most part, there is nothing subtle about work pressures. Bills need to be paid; our bosses or our businesses demand more and more time and concentration. On the other hand, there is the soft and gentle feel of our connection to our children. It is frighteningly easy to lose track of that subtle feeling, to let it slip away in the stress of keeping up on the job front. It is just as easy in the concentrated focus of work to lose track altogether of the markedly different patterns and rhythms of our children's lives.

Upon reflection, it's a wonder that so many of us—wonderfully skilled at figuring out the most intricate logical problems—can be so incredibly dense about something so crucially important to us as our children. So one Post-it note that should stay forever on your desk is that your children should be reminded constantly of how important your connection to them is. And the different ways available to us to do this are unlimited.

In strengthening our connection to our children while at work, one of the things we can do is to stop drawing such hard-and-fast lines between "work" and "home." We need to make room in our working lives for our children. Bring them to work occasionally, communicate with them from work on a regular basis, or simply take some time each working day to wonder where they are and what they are doing. Just opening those new channels binds us closer together and creates surprising possibilities.

Our emotional connection to our children is like an invisible umbilical cord. We need to maintain a constant flow of nourishment between us. And whether we live in the same house or thousands of miles away, the key ingredient is time—not physical presence, but real, focused, emotionally present time.

Make quality time

True presence, real time, is when we are fully emotionally engaged. It is when we can see our children from a state of wonder and enjoyment. It can take place in their physical presence, while talking to them on the telephone, or when writing them a letter. No matter how we accomplish it, it bathes and energizes them with a shower of our undivided love and attention.

True presence, real quality time, does not relate to what we are doing or where we are when we do it, but how we are doing it. When we are emotionally available to our children—wide open to whatever they need, welcoming and supportive of wherever they are—the easy and natural way of being forges the most pure and unbreakable bonds. It is so simple and yet so hard to remember.

With all our adult distractions, with all the pressures and obligations tugging for attention, it is easy for us to drift away, to compartmentalize our minds like a multitasking computer—one part thinking about a problem at work, one part worrying over how we are going to get the bills under control, another part trying to imagine some free time when we can relax, and still another part answering our children's questions. To our children, however, that particle of attention feels exactly like what it is—mental crumbs—and it feeds the distance between us.

We need to try very hard to be present with our children whenever we can and, if that is not possible, at least explain to them why. When you live a life that is packed to overflowing, you need to become proficient at twisting time to your needs. One way to stamp time with a special intensity is to be powerfully present.

Another way is to make use of stolen time. We all remember with exquisite joy the feeling of playing hooky—stealing time away from what we are supposed to be doing. Stolen time comes out of nowhere—it surprises and delights. Stolen time stretches out so that a few hours can seem wonderfully long. Stolen time is pure luxury; it exists solely for us to savor. When we share our stolen time with our children, we invite them into an exceedingly intimate and magical world, where our relationship to them is all that exists.

Whether we live in separate cities, are off on submarines for months at a time, or simply work too much, there is a very simple truth we need to incorporate into our fathering: distance is measured in neither miles, nor minutes, nor words, nor touch. The distance that matters is measured in our children's hearts. Our job is to be there—fully, powerfully, and always present in their hearts.

Know your children deeply

Who is this miracle? How much of the individual personality of an infant is in the genes, how much is learned behavior, and, for lack of a more descriptive word, how much comes from the soul of this tiny child? These are fascinating questions over which there seems to be endless debate among biologists, psychologists, social scientists, and theologians. From the viewpoint of parenthood, this is one of the great mysteries of life. For it is one thing to understand where babies come from, and quite another to understand where *this* baby came from.

We can all accept the notion that each of us is a unique individual, but sometimes it is difficult in practice to extend that acceptance comfortably all the way back to birth. This probably stems from our overemphasis of language: We are waiting for an explanation, whereas our preverbal children aren't waiting for anything. As adults, we feel seriously handicapped and emotionally deprived if we are unable to speak the language of infants and toddlers with any degree of skill. Some of us are lucky enough to get a crash course.

We also have a tendency to overestimate the effect of genetics. This is a kind of ego-driven blindness that can be particularly pernicious in parenting. From the obvious physical bequests of genetics—"he has my eyes" or "she has her mother's nose"—it is a short, wobbly, and usually very inaccurate step to "he's just like me" or "she's just like her mother." Suddenly, your poor child is saddled with all your habits, strengths, weaknesses, preferences, and peculiarities. That's a very heavy load for a child who can't even speak up in self-defense.

There we are, proudly projecting a very powerful image of how we see our children, and the message they receive is that this is what they are supposed to be, this is what will make Dad happy and proud. Because making us happy is so important to our children, they end up wasting an enormous amount of time and effort trying to cram themselves into the mold we created instead of exploring and developing who they truly are.

It is very easy to fall into this pit unwittingly, and the long-term results can be disastrous. This is one reason why it is so important for us as fathers to do our own emotional work. We must be very clear about who we are and what our needs are, and we must be certain that we do not unconsciously burden our children with our expectations. They are far too young and impressionable to sort out our expectations from their own, the things in life that interest and excite them.

Putting pressure on our children to be like us or, even worse, to be what we wanted to be but never quite succeeded at becoming, can be doubly handicapping. It does not matter what the expectation is: to love to read, to be outgoing and charming, to enjoy fishing, to succeed in business. Anything that we impose as a vision for their lives will more than likely set them up to fail, set us up for disappointment, and confuse and derail their own development.

Wanting our children—particularly our sons—to follow in our footsteps is an unconscious tendency that we fathers fall into with much greater regularity than mothers. Perhaps it is the tangible proof we seek that something of who we are has been passed on. Mothers, on the other hand, need only remember the powerfully intimate day of their child's birth. It may also be our concern that they "do something meaningful" with their lives, which we all too easily translate into doing what we did. Whatever the reason, it is a potentially dangerous trap that should be avoided consciously.

Learn from your children

One of the best "secrets" of parenting I know I learned from my daughter. She was seven at the time, and, out of the blue, she came up to me and said, "Ask me a question." So I asked, "Who's your boyfriend?" and she said, "Dad, I'm only seven." "Okay," I said, "Who's your best friend?" "Debbie," she replied. Right then and there, I realized that I didn't know that fundamental thing about her. Here was my beautiful, sweet daughter for whom I would die, and I didn't even know her best friend's name! For the next two hours, I acted like a kid, asking a million questions for every answer she gave me. She was giggling away, and I learned more about my daughter in those two hours than I had in seven years.

Most of us are pretty good at asking probing questions of strangers at cocktail parties or business functions. We learn early on that, when someone is interested enough in who you are to ask even somewhat revealing questions, most people, flattered by the interest, are more than willing to cooperate. Yet we rarely think to use this very simple and effective technique with our children. Maybe we get so burned out by their constant barrage of questions that we are afraid that asking even one tiny, little question will trigger a new avalanche. But that's just the kind of avalanche we need to be truly connected.

Here's is what I learned: The next time your children start asking you questions, start asking them questions right back. Think of it as loving revenge. We may have a lot more of the boring, practical answers they are after (How come hot water comes out when you turn the red handle and not the blue handle?), but they have a lot more of the answers we are really interested in. What do they want to be when they grow up? What makes them happy? What is their most favorite thing? Their most favorite place? If they could go anywhere in the world, where would it be? If they could do anything, what would it be? If they could be anyone, who would they be? If they ran the world, what rules would they have? What changes would they make? What makes them sad? Angry? What's their favorite color/animal/song/television show? And for every answer you get, ask why.

Be their personal storyteller

One of the greatest untapped resources of fathering is our ability to tell stories. Storytelling is in our bones. From man's earliest days, huddled around campfires, it was through storytelling that we passed on information and taught the next generation. It is still one of the most powerful tools at our disposal, and one that our children love.

In the telling of stories, we create new worlds that capture our children's interest and invite their participation. Great stories have been used throughout history to teach, but they can be just as important as a tool for building and reaffirming connection. The new and exciting world of interactive CD-ROMs and video games can't hold a candle to the interpersonal, interactive capacity of storytelling. We can create a context, a situation, bring it to a point of decision, and then invite our children to choose a path. With that, we have them invested in the world of our story. Then we get to twist them around in our fantasy world, asking them again to make choices, take risks, and, most important, stretch their imaginations and have fun. And we are doing it together.

Fantasies, historical sagas, moral tales, wild and crazy adventures, scary stories, mysteries, stories without endings, stories without purpose—it is in the telling, the listening, the imagining, the squealing, hugging, screaming, and laughing that we weave deep and beautiful connections with our children. And it is in those magical moments of sharing that we get glimpses into the deepest parts of who they are.

Ride the roller coaster of adolescence

If you think connecting with your infant is a challenge in today's day and age, just wait until they get to be teenagers. It may help to remember that adolescence truly is a tough time for our children. They are passing through many very confusing doorways. They need to leave the helpless humiliation of childhood behind and lay the groundwork for an adult identity—and it isn't easy, particularly with Dad and Mom hanging over their shoulder. Our teenagers' sudden interest in privacy and their lack of subtlety should not be taken personally, but it does require some adaptation. Because if we don't adapt to it, we can quickly find ourselves very much outside their lives, right when we may be more needed than ever.

Although it is important to respect their need for more autonomy, it is critical that they know we are every bit as interested in their lives and committed to knowing, understanding, and supporting them as we have ever been. The process of inquiry simply needs to become more sophisticated, the communication methods more mature. Ask better questions, those that can't be answered with one word. Be willing to ask now and be answered later. Ask more questions about what they think and believe and feel, and respect their answers, even if you don't agree.

One of the most effective ways to get our children—particularly teenagers—to reveal themselves to us is to reveal ourselves to them. Tell them stories about your life—about things you worried about, mistakes you made, about being confused, being scared, taking risks. Tell them funny stories and sad stories, incidents that came out all right and those that were a disaster. The message is that they are important enough to know these intimate details of your life, that even their father had to go through these things. Show them that you survived difficulties as a child, and they will too. When we are courageous enough to reveal to our children the unwashed stories about ourselves, it gives them the comfort of knowing that they can reveal themselves to us without fear.

As a friend of mine once said, "Kids are a flat-out gas." As fathers, we need to hold on to that truth with great consistency. Truly, deeply, enthusiastically enjoying our children is one of the fundamental building blocks of an enriching lifelong connection.

Often, all we need do to really enjoy our children is remember that this opportunity to be with and interact with them is not work, but rather what we work for. When we approach each interaction with our children as a close encounter of the most fascinating kind, we are rarely disappointed.

Follow their lead

Enjoying your children can be like that compelling novel that you can't put down and can't wait to pick up again. Their days are filled with wonder and excitement, and all we need to do to become captivated by the unfolding drama of their lives is allow ourselves to be drawn into their world as much as we can. Get involved in their studies, pay attention to what they are learning, to what bores them and what excites them. Allow yourself to be fascinated by the choices they make and to wonder what is around the next bend.

Sometimes, little things crop up that take the fun out of our interactions with our children—their not enjoying an activity we do, arguments over money, fussiness, whatever. When that happens, we need to change the dynamic—and as soon as possible. Usually, there is a simple and obvious solution, if we don't get caught up in the conflict. Change your schedule, change the activity, do whatever you can to change whatever has become the obstacle to sheer enjoyment: stop playing one-on-one if your daughter is tired of losing (or let her win); stop swimming at the Y every day for exercise when your kids hate the water; take some outings close to home (or stay home!) if car trips always result in stress. Some things can't be changed, and giving up for the sake of our children all the things we enjoy is no solution either. But for every stuck situation we encounter, there are invariably numerous alternatives that can be employed to the enjoyment of everyone.

As fathers, we are doing great if we manage to stay on our feet while we madly maneuver to keep close to our kids. We can't afford to let obstacles slow us down, so we have to be sure that our time with our children is truly and mutually enjoyable. From that point, everything else will flow. One wonderful way to accomplish this is to let our children teach us all over again how to play.

An odd thing happens when you grown up: you start being more concerned with results and less concerned with the process of arriving at them. There are many explanations for this, not the least of which is that, in a world that elevates money to god-like significance, the result—the product, the sale, the price tag, the payoff—is all-important. In this arena, our children have much to teach us. For them, it is the journey that is most important—how something is done, the actual process, the interactions along the way—and arriving at the destination is just the icing on the cake.

One morning some years ago when I was visiting the ocean, I took a walk along the beach and saw a father and two small children with buckets and shovels, excavating a huge area for a sand castle. They all seemed to be having a great time, laughing and running around. Later that afternoon, I returned and saw the children wandering around picking up seashells while their father was still hard at work, trying to complete the sand castle. By sunset, the kids and their mother had disappeared back into the beach house, and Dad was just putting the crowning touches on the castle.

In its own way, this story is a poignant commentary on how easy it is to get fixated on results. I am sure, had he thought about it, this father would have said that spending time with his children was more important than finishing a sand castle that was going to be washed away with the night tide anyway. But he didn't think about it. He started building and, by god, he wasn't going to stop until it was finished.

When we play with our children, we need to throw our expectations overboard and turn control over to the play experts—our kids. Playing need not be about teaching, about solving problems, or about building something. Watch any toddler: The best part about building a tower is knocking it down. Playing should be about enjoying ourselves, and it is an art form at which children are extraordinarily talented. Let them take the lead, but also be willing to invite them into your play.

Don't ever assume

When it comes to siblings, don't ever assume that what you learned from the first will apply to the second. Our children may share with each other a lot of DNA and environmental influences, but it is rare indeed to find siblings who are at all alike. It is almost as though the first thing a newborn does is check out any existing brothers or sisters and set about becoming as different from them as possible. Raising one child certainly gives us many of the skills and much of the confidence we need to make fathering a second or third child a little easier; but in the most important areas—the ability to truly know and deeply connect with our children—it can be more of an obstacle than an aid. We get lazy, think we know more than we do, and make assumptions based on past experience.

Each of our children is extraordinarily unique. And though we may have that "I've done this before" swagger, we haven't done this before with this child—no matter what "this" is. Learning how to understand and communicate with different children is very much like learning different languages. Some kids you can't shut up, and others you can't get to talk. Some are wound-up energy machines, while others are calm and reflective. Some are highly sensitive to what is going on around them, whereas others are completely oblivious to everything but what they are doing. Some kids would watch television from morning to night if you let them, while others couldn't care less. They talk differently, move differently, feel differently, see the world differently.

Our children give us so much, and one of their most surprising and welcome gifts are the doors they open to us that were never open to us before. Through our children's differences, interests, and passions, we can enter foreign worlds and experience whole new ways of relating that are completely mysterious to us. When our children are like us in one way or another, it provides an avenue of connection that is simple and easy. When our children are not like us at all, however, it can be intimidating. We feel helpless in the fathering role with which we are most comfortable—that of teacher and guide. What do we have to offer? We can't teach, because we don't know; we can't resolve the problems they come across, because the context is unfamiliar.

This can be a painful dilemma, but, in truth, it is an extraordinary opportunity. Often, what our children need, what they ask of us, is to forget teaching and problem-solving, leave the preconceived roles of fathering behind, and simply be with them in the moment, share this place that is their lives. Let them know that, even though you are different, their interests, dreams, trials, and heartbreaks are important to you.

The very fact that they are different from us is one of the great gifts of fathering. Together, with and through our children, we can open ourselves to discovery, to learning, to expanding our appreciation of those different from us, and we can do this without great emotional risk. They stretch our boundaries and contribute to our growth.

5

Modeling

This fathering business is just not as simple as we all wish it were. Our guts tell us that, if we truly love our children, everything else will sort itself out. Unfortunately, it doesn't always work out that way. Loving our children is undeniably the essential starting point, but we can't just sit back comfortably, knowing how much we love them, and expect everything to turn out all right. Our love for our children may be the fiber from which our relationship is woven, but we still must show it. And it must shine through in bold, vibrant colors.

Father with respect and honesty

One important thread in this tapestry is what we live and teach about respect. For many men, the word itself is very charged. It is often used and misused in anger, but the concept plays a central role in a well-lived life. One reason it is so difficult to become completely comfortable with the concept of respect is that embedded within it are two distinctly different components that exist in a state of constant tension. For respect is a word of both connection and disconnection.

On the one hand, respect is the ultimate expression of our connection to one another in its most basic form—the regard we hold for all living things, simply because they are a part of the miracle of life. In that way, respect is given like the love we hold for our children, without conditions.

But respect also connotes distinctions between people, the fundamental measuring stick we use to separate the people we admire from those we don't. That kind of respect is conditional, based on the development of and adherence to a strong, individual moral code. From this place, we make judgments of others' behavior.

It is from the first, broader aspect of respect that most of our fathering must flow. We must respect the individuality of our children, their unlimited potential, and, always, their feelings. But it is the second kind of respect about which we must teach them, and through much more than just our words. It is our responsibility to teach our children the more complicated lessons of respect—about exercising moral judgment and making difficult choices—by our own example. As the old saying goes, actions speak louder than words.

When we become fathers, we are not asked to place an order for the kind of child we want. They may be athletic or total klutzes, intellectual or academic underachievers, charming and outgoing or contemplative and shy, tall, short, gifted, or handicapped. Whatever unique combination we are given, they are our children; if we cannot respect them for who they are instead of who we may want them to be, it is our great failing, but our children will pay the price.

Respect is the acceptance and honoring of who the other person truly is. One way we can demonstrate that respect for our children is to remember the power of fathering, and to walk softly when we are in their world. At work, we are often rewarded for having firm and definitive opinions, but in their arena, we need to remember that our opinions carry the weight of gods, and that can be very difficult for our children to bear gracefully. We may think their choice of TV programs or music or books is boring and uninteresting, but that does not give us the right to announce it or, worse still, denounce them.

One of the time-honored roles of fathers is to be windows to the world for our children. In fulfilling that role, we need to expose them to a broad range of interests and not restrict them by the boundaries we've chosen for ourselves. In that task, we are certainly aided by the rapid development of entertainment and communications media, but we are challenged at the same time. Our children are not growing up in the same world we grew up in. For better and for worse, they are exposed to a much broader and, in some ways, a much harsher array of influences than we were at their age. We need to accept, appreciate, and work with the scope of that exposure and, at the same time, make sure that it does not become a substitute for our participation.

Bad television is an invitation to good discussion. News of war, natural disasters, or the ranting of posturing politicians is an opportunity for meaningful dialog. Invite your children to participate in "serious" adult conversations whenever and in whatever manner seems appropriate. Ask their thoughts and opinions about the issues that arise, and treat their opinions with respect, even if you disagree. Respecting their opinions means it is alright to question gently why they hold a particular view, and you can certainly offer your own thoughts in as provisional a manner as possible. But it is not alright to say, "I completely disagree." Coming from Dad, that is tantamount to telling them they are stupid.

Transitions are always tough. When our children are very young, we make all the rules and enforce them because it is necessary and because they need to know that we are there, setting boundaries and limits. Eventually, the time comes for that authority to be handed over. It is no longer necessary or appropriate for us to make their rules, no longer our job to impose our boundaries and our limits. We can no longer protect them from themselves. Our (hopefully fully prepared) children must begin assuming command and control over their own destinies.

In the process of making this awkward and poignant transition with our children, we are forced to grapple with the second kind of respect, the conditional respect we hold for those we believe live their lives honestly, responsibly, and with integrity. We will always love and respect our children because they are our children. As they assume more and more control over their lives, they learn that, as adults, respect is conditional, that it must be earned.

Ironically, one of the notions about fathering that has gotten badly twisted as it was handed down through the generations is that we deserve respect because we are fathers. Nothing could be further from the truth. We deserve respect as fathers only if we earn it—by demonstrating that we are good fathers. We are the adults, and we are responsible and accountable for our actions.

We can't expect to teach our children lessons by which we refuse to live. "Do as I say and not as I do" won't cut it. We can't smoke, overeat, drink too much, ignore our health, and work too much and under too stressful conditions, and then expect our children to refrain from self-destructive behavior. They may choose different drugs or behaviors, but we will have been the model, and any objection on our part will be seen by them as the height of hypocrisy.

At the heart of this issue is the fundamental importance of always being honest with our children. Depending on the issue being discussed and the age of the children, that may involve a more-or-less complete answer. It may even involve a straightforward but honest refusal to discuss issues that you believe, for one reason or another, are not appropriate (like details of your sex life). What's important is that they know that what you do say to them can be trusted.

The importance of establishing that trusting bond of honesty cannot be overestimated. Without it, our children are set adrift without moorings. If you can't trust your own parents, who in the world can you trust? Being scrupulously honest with our children lets them know that we trust them with the truth. It also inoculates them against one of life's most vicious scourges: people who bend or twist the truth in order to manipulate others.

Our children are very good at knowing when we are telling the truth. Remember, we have been godlike creatures with seemingly awesome powers for most of their lives, and they have put some of that time to use, studying our moves and trying to understand and anticipate our thoughts and actions. We forget that, as well as we know our children, in many respects they know us even better. They may not have an adult understanding of who we are, but they are meticulous students of what we do.

It is our actions more than our words that set into stone the patterns that most dramatically influence our children's lives. If we break our promises, even about what may seem to us to be small things, such as showing up at baseball practice or a school play, we show them that they are not very important and that broken promises are an acceptable part of life.

Nowhere is this more true than in our relationship to their mothers. If you are still living with their mother, you are modeling how a man and woman should be together. The nature and quality of that relationship will be the model toward which your children will gravitate when they are ready to marry.

At the same time, we can't engage in constant verbal battles with our wives without expecting our children to think that this is what marriage will be like. We cannot treat our wives disrespectfully without expecting our sons to model our behavior in their own marriages and our daughters to expect it from their husbands. We cannot silently suffer an unhappy marriage without expecting to pass on our legacy of misery to our children.

If you are separated or divorced, the way you interact with your children's mother will be the microscope under which what you say about honesty and respect will be examined. What you cannot control does not matter—whether the divorce was amiable or contentious, whether your ex-wife is the most cooperative soul or the most vindictive, mean-spirited person in the world. What you can control, and therefore the only thing that truly matters, is how you act and what you say.

Our children possess a remarkable trait—they are able to recognize and gravitate toward that which resonates as most sincere and true. If we act respectfully and responsibly, if we behave toward our ex-wives with dignity, integrity, and compassion, ultimately that will be the lesson our children incorporate into their lives. Sometimes it is difficult, particularly if your ex-wife is actively trying to undermine or obstruct your relationship with your children. Sometimes it feels hopeless, especially if the children get dragged into an ex-wife's divisive manipulations. But if we want to be good fathers, it is not optional behavior. The legacy of respect we pass on to our children has more to do with who we are and how we act than what we say.

Balance challenge and acceptance

Good fathering is not simple. You can't just follow a script or a set of rules, and much of what you must do seems to involve constant tension from opposite directions. One place where that tension can surface on a daily basis is in our role as teachers or coaches. It is our job to encourage our children to take risks, to expand their world, to expose themselves to new experiences; yet, at the same time, it is our sacred duty to support them simply for who they are. Though it's easy to err in either direction, men often find themselves more in the pushing-and-prodding dimension than women do. We may have experienced this with our own fathers and should struggle to avoid doing the same to our kids, particularly our sons.

In reality, there is less tension between support and challenge than it may seem at times, because this base of unconditional support is what makes it possible for us to effectively and lovingly challenge our children to take risks. If we remember and express our love, if we follow our hearts, we will know what to do in a given circumstance—whether to push or hold back.

Our children need to know that we love them simply because they are our children. They can make mistakes, be scared and cry, lose every spelling bee or race, strike out in the bottom of the ninth with the winning runs on base, disobey, think bad thoughts, or spill their milkshake all over the backseat of the new car—and Dad will still love them.

That unmovable, unshakable, unconditional love must be as solid as a mountain of granite and as reliable as the sun rising every morning. With that foundation, our children are free to attempt the daunting array of seemingly daredevil feats that make up the daily challenge of growing up—free to take risks, to explore their world and their interests, to dream of running like the wind or soaring like an eagle; free to daydream, to collect pebbles or bugs, to wonder what they will do when they grow up; free to invent games and change the rules, and to make up imaginary worlds and populate them with imaginary friends; free to dream themselves into lofty positions of power and respect; free to change dreams as often as they change T-shirts.

If our love is conditional, our children will feel as though their very lives are built on shifting sands. All of their energy will be focused outward, on trying to solve the mystery of what they must do to be loved by Dad. Instead of spending their time exploring and experimenting with the raw material of their own personality, they become obsessed with studying our every move and mood shift, the better to anticipate what they must do to please us.

If we fail them here, by not providing a solid foundation of unconditional love, they grow up so outwardly focused that they lose track of their own desires. They forget their dreams or, worse still, forget how to dream. They never discover who they are and what they need in order to be happy. They lose or never find the unique trajectory of their lives, becoming instead like satellites, always captured in the gravitational pull of some other body.

In this most basic function, it is not enough that we love our children unconditionally—we must let them know it over and over again. One way we do that is to clearly separate their endeavors and achievements from their being. Encourage them and support them in the things they do, but love them for the beautiful little people they are. For many of us, trained as we were in the male world of achievement, this is more difficult than it seems. We are very comfortable commending effort or celebrating a job well done, but aren't always that practiced at just weaving a strong, soft web of love.

When we become fathers, we assume a position of natural authority that will last for nearly two decades. We are bigger, stronger, and wiser than our children. We have the knowledge and experience of countless life lessons, and much of their whirlwind of energy is dedicated to soaking up as much of that precious information as possible. What our children need from us is access to our years of experience. What they do not need is a live-in know-it-all. Difficult as this may be sometimes, we need to become comfortable with our role as the elder statesman—without ego involvement and without needing to supply all the answers. We don't know everything; as a matter of fact, if they had a clue as to how little we do know, they wouldn't be angry, they'd be terrified.

We must learn how to provide our children with the information that's necessary and the information that is asked for, without interfering with their sense of wonder and experimentation and without encouraging their natural inclination to believe that we know more than we actually do. We can help them understand, we can coach them in ways to approach problems, we can encourage them to take risks, and we can pass on what wisdom we have gained from our experiences—but it must be an offering, not a demand. Our children don't need us to have answers for every question; they don't need us to be infallible superheroes. They may at times imagine us in this light, but what they really need from us is the benefit of our experience, buttressed by our unconditional love, untainted honesty, unfailing support, and unswerving encouragement.

The best lessons are those we learn by ourselves. We know this, god how we know this—and yet it is so easy to fall prey to the temptation of always supplying answers. Sometimes, it is our own childish need to show that we know the answer: Our child asks a question, and we suddenly feel ourselves back in school, our hand waving frantically in the air: I know! I know the answer! At other times, it is just an overwhelming desire to fix the problem.

Unfortunately (or fortunately), life must be lived, and we cannot hand down our wisdom and experience as a complete package. There are ways, however, to use our knowledge efficiently to lead, nudge, entice, and prod our children to their own experiences. By knowing our children very well, by paying close attention to their rapidly changing concerns, we can become reliable and effective coaches. We can encourage them in directions we believe will enrich their lives; we can anticipate and identify issues that they will need to ponder; we can help them analyze situations that seem confusing and articulate their feelings; and we can show them how understanding those feelings is the compass that will lead them to seeing more clearly.

We can do all this without supplying the answers and without taking over. In the process, we will add to, instead of detract from, the self-confidence our children need to meet life's challenges.

When our children run into roadblocks, what they need most from us is understanding and empathy. Because we are so used to solving problems in our working environment, it is very easy for us just to jump to the solution quickly and efficiently. Unfortunately, that approach can undermine instead of help. What's worse, it means losing a golden opportunity to support and connect with our children at the deepest level. If we are to be good coaches for our children, we need to know when to be supportive, when to prod and encourage, when to advise and analyze, and when to simply offer understanding.

At any given moment, there will always be a specific "problem," but in a larger and much more important sense, the real issue with which our children are grappling is how to analyze and come up with their own solutions. The specific issues will always sort themselves out—with or without our help; it is the skill and confidence to sort out their own problems that our children really need, and it is there that our energy should be focused.

Not surprisingly, at the heart of good coaching is feeling. We need to understand and empathize with our children's feelings. Often, that is all they need from us. Growing up can be very frustrating. Our children must feel as if they are navigating through treacherous and mystifying waters without any of the tools or resources they need to succeed. What they require more than anything is for us to provide the emotional safety net that will give them the strength and courage to persevere. They need to be able to rely upon us to support them without judgment when they falter, to encourage and assure them when they grow timid or confused, and to assist and advise them when they ask for it.

Who you are and what you do matter

Mahatma Gandhi said it best: "You must be the change you want to see in the world." His words speak powerfully to parents concerned about raising healthy children. In order for our children to have a strong sense of self, we must have one ourselves—and model it for them.

This is not an area where you can do for your children what you couldn't do for yourself. Just as they will dismiss your lectures on the evils of smoking if they see you puffing through two packs a day, so anything positive you say will be drowned out by your negative example. After all, if their own parents couldn't stand up for themselves, couldn't find the strength or courage to live their lives fully and courageously, then how can they possibly imagine that they could succeed?

If, for example, we, consciously or unconsciously, behave in ways that demonstrate a lack of respect for a woman's capacity to take charge of her own life, how can we expect our own children to overcome the weight of that prejudice? It is one of the great, and certainly one of the most difficult, gifts of parenting that, to do the best by our children, we must first stretch and grow to bring out the best in ourselves.

Take care of yourself

If you want the your children to grow up strong and fearless, ready to take on life with confidence and passion, then you must show them that it can be done. In the ongoing struggle to balance your personal life and your roles as spouse and parent, it is surprisingly easy to sacrifice your own needs until there is little left but taking care of others. From afar, it may seem a noble undertaking, but the message that gets passed on to our children is that it is a good thing to ignore your own needs to serve others.

As you master the art of nourishing your children's self-esteem, you will undoubtedly become aware of some of your own, or your spouse's, unmet needs. Today, far too many women are well-trained caregivers, giving their best to their family and work, yet all too frequently ignoring their own needs. In the process of championing our children, we feel that it's imperative to do all that we can to foster their sense of self-worth. Yet it is often rare that we do the same for ourselves.

Our children learn by example, so don't expect your children to do for themselves what you won't do for yourself. If you want them to take care of themselves, feel good about themselves, and passionately pursue their interests, they must see you being fully engaged in your own life.

Whether it is regular exercise, reading books, starting your own business, being politically active, treating yourself regularly to some self-nurturing activities, or just carving out time for self-reflection, daily meditation, or journal keeping, by your example, you model the value of self-nurturing for your children.

Live fearlessly

Fear is both an essential human emotion and a crippling disease. Without fear, it is highly unlikely we would have made it this far as a species, but in many ways, it was a lot simpler back in the days of "fight or flight." In the incredibly complex world we live in today, we are reminded on an almost constant basis that we are not in control. Tragedy unfolds every evening on the nightly news; the media convince us that we are surrounded by senseless violence. We can see with our own eyes the poverty and suffering in the world. Even purely accidental occurrences can strike at us from nowhere. Planes and automobiles crash, loved ones get sick and die. Hurtful things happen, and there is no way for us to protect against them.

It is small wonder, then, that so many people, at different times in their lives, become almost paralyzed by fear. However, when that happens, we cease being ourselves. We lose the strength and courage to live our lives the way we want to and our very selves begin to shrink. Ironically, we begin to inflict upon ourselves the very pain from which we are ineffectively trying to protect ourselves.

We cannot expect our children to have the courage to face their own fears and the strength of character to rise above them if we cannot lead the way. Fear will always be with us; we fear failing, and we sometimes even fear succeeding. We may be afraid that people won't like us or, worse, that our loved ones will stop loving us. Fear we cannot avoid, but we can make a concerted effort to keep it from controlling our behavior.

It's OK for our children to see us being afraid, if they also see us being willing to move through that fear to embrace what we truly want in the world. In that way, they learn that the way through life is *through*, or, as Susan Jeffers says in her best-selling book, "Feel the fear and do it anyway."

Celebrate your successes

Raising children is one of the most difficult things anyone can possibly undertake. Not just because it is so time consuming, or even because it is so energetically intense. What makes it such a continuously difficult job is that, by the very nature of the undertaking, the rules are never the same. Being a parent is like being on a rapidly moving conveyor belt and trying to keep track of and properly respond to a collection of movies being projected all around you.

When we begin, we are relatively young (for the most part), wholly inexperienced, and absorbed in the helpless squirming of our baby. Then, in a frighteningly short period of time, we are older and, we hope, wiser and watching our young adult move into life. Between those two milestones, the landmarks change daily and sometimes hourly; we must constantly reassess how much reassurance and protection our children need, how much challenge and discipline, how much responsibility they are ready for, how deep a truth they can hear.

At every moment, we must evaluate and try to respond in a way that fits their needs at that moment, that reassures them at the same time it stretches them. We must remind them of the things they need to remember, while at the same time honoring them for the strength and initiative they have assumed. We must open them to the world in a way that allows them to experience their own power and competence without setting them up to fail. Being a parent requires the wisdom of Solomon, the patience of Job, and the dexterity of a professional juggler, and we will fall short more often than we will ever want to admit.

So when it does work, when you can see, feel, and experience the powerful resonance of a moment well handled, when the connection between you and your children has that almost tangible throb, take the time to relish your success, to appreciate the artistry in that moment, the delicate balancing act that you have pulled off with such elegance.

We must remember not only that we are learning and that we can do this well, but that doing so presents an image to our children of flawed, but still competent and confident, adults. And because that image is so true, it gives them the permission they need to make mistakes and still be proud of their accomplishments. By tracking our successes (and those of our children), we construct or repair a healthy sense of self-esteem.

Own up to your mistakes

Self-esteem isn't some quality we're born with, or that we have to develop before we're out of preschool or it's too late. Strong self-esteem is like a good bank account that is built up over time, and can always be bolstered. If, like most of us, you've made your share of mistakes with your children, don't panic—just start now to make up for the past. And this applies to your own self-esteem too. Knowing that you may not have done all that you could have for your child is a blow to *your* self-esteem. You can begin to turn that around immediately by acknowledging the times you've made mistakes with your child. It takes a strong sense of self-esteem to admit a mistake; adults with low self-esteem avoid it because they can't stand the sense of inadequacy it creates.

Showing your children that you have the sensitivity and wisdom to recognize that you were wrong, and the strength of self to apologize for it, is not only a powerful example. It also dramatically illustrates just how important they are. After all, from their perspective, an adult apologizing to a kid is downright earthshaking.

At the same time, it is a wonderful object lesson in how people should treat each other. To our children, it often seems as if they spend half their time grudgingly apologizing for what really amounts to the everyday excesses of growing up. So to hear a sincere apology from an adult puts the entire exercise on a whole different level. It's no longer just "I did something wrong and had to say I was sorry"; it suddenly becomes clear that everyone should be held to certain standards of behavior and that adults are not the only members of the species who are deserving of respect.

Asking for their help, as in "If I ever make you feel bad like that again, please tell me," reinforces the message that they deserve to be treated respectfully and that they are capable enough to help you do it right. But be sure to back up your promises; nothing undermines a child's confidence quite as much as an erratic and unreliable parent. By modeling the art of apologizing, you teach them a real skill. Admitting mistakes takes courage, and your children will be profoundly moved by your efforts.

Live deeply, no matter what you do

It's easy to get caught up in the hurried flow of life, but when we do, we run the risk of skimming over the more meaningful moments and opportunities that could allow us to experience our lives in their complete richness and fullness. After all, at the end of our lives, it will not be how much we got done, how many "to do" lists we got through, or how much money we accumulated that will matter. What will be important is the depth to which we lived our own lives and the extent to which we positively impacted the lives of others.

Begin early by sharing with your children the traditions and rituals of your childhood, and then deepen them by tailoring them to what seems to fit your own family. They'll remember these special occasions for the rest of their lives. They will become part of your family folklore, the story of your family, and they will recreate it for their own kids. By feeling part of a long family tradition and taking part in the flow of that continuum, you give your children a great blessing. To become a part of such a ritualized tradition gives them a feeling of connectedness that will continue to nourish them their whole lives and will expand their sense of belonging.

Don't forget the food! Preparing meals is such a powerfully symbolic connection. It is how we nurture one another, how we surprise and please, how we survive, how we give the gift of life each and every day. Welcome your children into the kitchen, that magical place of love and history. When the special foods are prepared for the celebratory feasts your family may make at Thanksgiving, Passover, or Chinese New Year, invite them into the kitchen, and introduce them into a kind of ancient "mystery." Involve them in each stage, from the planning, preparing, decorating, cooking, and serving to the feasting itself. It will make them a part of the great circle of giving and receiving that makes a family strong.

Practice kindness

When we talk about self-esteem, we think immediately of things like strength, empowerment, confidence, having the courage of our convictions—big powerful words that paint a picture of our children as having the resources to go out into the world and meet whatever challenges may come. We don't immediately think of kindness, partly because kindness has a softer, sweeter feel to it. It's almost as if kindness were a nice thing, but not something we think of as powerful. We couldn't be more wrong.

Going out of your way to make other people comfortable and feel good about themselves actually has a double impact on young children. First, they get to see firsthand, through your example, just how easy it is to be a positive force in the world. In and of itself, this can be an invaluable lesson, simply because, in the much smaller world they inhabit, young children can easily find themselves feeling powerless and ineffectual. Just seeing the adults in their lives bringing smiles and satisfaction to others is a constant reminder of the depth of power we all carry with us every day of our lives.

At the same time, it can be a direct benefit when we turn our praise on our children. Not only will they directly hear the compliments, but they will be more inclined to take them to heart, because it is in character; they realize "This is the way Dad is," instead of thinking "Oh Dad's just saying that to try to make me feel good." Sincere praise helps build self-esteem because it is an articulated acknowledgment of their value and importance. But our children are nobody's fools, and if they are the only ones getting the praise, it won't take them long to figure out that there is something insincere about our efforts.

Practicing kindness is also a way to encourage our children by example to be positive about other people, and not to be shy about expressing enthusiasm. They will experience the power of positively affecting another person, and that power will come back to them many-fold, since everybody loves to be around people who make them feel good about themselves.

Don't be a hypocrite

It's almost inevitable that children will experiment to some degree with smoking, drugs, or alcohol, and the extent and the seriousness of that experimentation will be influenced significantly by your own behavior. This is a scary area for parents, because we don't even want to think about our children getting caught up in that quagmire, but it doesn't help if we try to avoid thinking or talking about it.

The first and most important issue we must all address is our own relationship to the instruments of addiction: alcohol, drugs (and that includes "prescription" drugs), and tobacco. Like anything else, what we do will have a much more profound effect than what we say—particularly if the two are in conflict. Certainly, if we are telling our children to avoid alcohol while we are regularly drinking to excess in their presence, both the message and the messenger are discredited. If we try to talk to them about being reasonable and responsible for their health by avoiding cigarettes while smoking two packs a day, our words will become the measure of our own hypocrisy.

At the same time, we can overdo the warnings to the point of losing all credibility. Alcohol in moderation plays an important role in our social and cultural tradition. Trying to characterize it as evil incarnate will likely end up convincing our children we have gone round the bend, and they'd rather go have a beer with some friends. Lumping all drug use together in one extremely dangerous and evil category can easily backfire. Drugs aren't equally dangerous. If you skip over that point, someone else will inform them of that fact, and everything you've said can be washed away in a moment. Children who are well informed in advance about the real effects and consequences of drugs and who have strong self-esteem are most effective in resisting the peer pressure involved with using drugs. But it won't help if the information is incorrect, or our behavior is inconsistent.

Smoking is an unmitigated health hazard from which any sane person will run. At the same time, it is deeply embedded in our society. As an ex-smoker (who can freely admit that I love the taste of a good cigarette), I know well how hard it is to reconcile the fact that smoking has no redeeming social value with the millions of people who are completely hooked. If you smoke and care about your children, stop. If you don't smoke, resist being overly harsh in your judgment, but at the same time be open and clear about the truth of any of your addictions.

Give them mentors and role models

This used to be a lot easier. Until very recently, children were not as isolated as they are today. Instead, they grew up surrounded by grandparents, aunts, uncles, friends from the neighborhood. But as we have become more affluent, families have become more isolated. The only adults to whom children are routinely exposed are their parents. That both puts inordinate pressure on us as parents and deprives our children of the broad spectrum of resources that they need to blossom.

When we live in small, insular nuclear families, we deprive our children of contact with the wide variety of humanity with which the world is graced, and their options for *becoming* are narrowed. But when we expose them to a wide variety of adult friends and relatives, they see many options for themselves: Oh, maybe I'll be a deep-sea diver like Uncle Jacques, or the head of a fashion studio like my mom's friend Stephanie. Self-image is created from a wide variety of sources, including role models. By providing them with actual role models (as opposed to images on TV), you give them a more accurate picture of adulthood.

Every adult in a child's life models behavior for them and teaches them in some way how to be in the world. A positive "presence" by any adult boosts a child's self-esteem, showing them they are important. As the African saying goes, it really does "take a village to raise a child." It's up to you to help find your child's village!

Support; don't direct

Children are such energetic and eager learning machines that it is very easy for us to get dragged into believing that we are somehow in charge of directing their growth and development—somehow "molding" them. We aren't and we shouldn't be. Yes, we need to provide guidance, establish limits, and encourage their sampling of a wide range of interests. But we should always remain attuned to their lives, their needs, and their interests, not our own.

Ultimately, what our children need from us most is to be acknowledged and loved for who they are. This is a sacred undertaking. If we do it well, we provide them with lasting comfort. We send them into the world knowing they are not alone, with confidence and a sense of self-worth that allows them to live their lives fully and joyfully. If we do it poorly, we send them out into the world lacking the confidence and self-esteem to identify and pursue what is necessary and important to them.

One of our deepest human needs is to be truly known and truly loved. That's why dedicating ourselves to learning who our children are and loving them for their own uniqueness is our most basic duty to them. If we fail, we send a message, intended or not, that they are not worthy: if your own father could not or would not take the time to really get to know you, then surely there must be nothing of value to know. It is a sacred duty, but it is also one of life's greatest pleasures—children are like an endless Christmas present.

Beginning on their day of birth and continuing throughout our lives, we are privileged to be an intimate part of the never-ending unfolding of a human being. To do it right, we need to remember that we are a part of a very complicated and intense learning process. Our children start by learning how to control their bodies—how to grasp, how to crawl, how to walk. They quickly progress to learning sophisticated human skills, from talking, abstract thinking, and identifying and expressing emotions to the intricate human dance of interaction. The more skilled they get, the better able they are to understand and clearly articulate who they are and what particular combination of desires, passions, dreams, and needs makes them unique.

We are given the great honor of participating in this blossoming and, if we do our part well, we can be an invaluable resource in helping, encouraging, supporting, and guiding them. But from our very adult perspective, we must remember that, at the heart of this adventure, is their learning, their discovering, their coming to full, vibrant consciousness of who they are.

On this journey, we do not and cannot have the answers. However, by watching our children with fascination as their answers emerge, by eagerly questioning them about how they feel, what they think, what interests them, we show them that their journey of discovery is tremendously important to us. Through our avid interest, we communicate to our children that truly, deeply knowing them is a source of great joy in our lives.

Use the power of words

The old saying "Sticks and stones may break my bones but words will never hurt me" is a big lie. Words can wound—terminally. By the time we become adults, we have usually long forgotten the extraordinary power of words. We live in a world so crammed full of words that we are only reminded of their impact when someone important to us carelessly says something hurtful.

But from the moment of birth, our children are soaking up messages from the world around them. From their still-new and fresh exposure to the magic of language, the impact and effect of words, especially those from their parents and other caregivers, are profoundly deep.

Children very quickly learn to judge themselves through the words, attitudes, and treatment of others. They develop their self-images through what they are told about themselves, and they learn self-worth from what others say to them or about them in their presence. Self-esteem can be strongly bolstered or torn into tatters simply by the verbal responses they receive to the things that they do. That's why one of the most important things you can do for the children in your life is to remember that you are a polished and penetrating mirror. Everything you say and do is reflected back to them, from infancy on, with laser-like intensity.

Babies must be provided with an enjoyable, warm, responsive environment of close bonding, including the innate language of "parentese." From the time they are born, start telling your children that you love them, and don't ever stop. A toddler depends solely on family and caregivers for the words that will either build or destroy confidence and esteem. A child who is building an understanding of language is also developing a new way of understanding itself. And always, the words spoken to them must match the true feelings of the speaker, just as actions must match attitudes, so that the child learns to trust what is said to them. Telling a child that it is important and that you love them while you are preoccupied with three other tasks doesn't do that little soul justice.

What we say and how we say it have the power to do good or harm. To love them well, to be an example for them, we must choose and use our words very carefully.

Share your emotions

When my daughter was very young, I used to tell her lots of stories about when I was a child. What I learned very quickly was that the stories she loved most always involved me screwing up, getting into trouble, or emotionally imploding. Every time we got around to storytelling, my daughter would scream out, "Tell the one about how you cried when you didn't get a horse for Christmas!" or "Tell the one where you threw up on Grandpa's best suit!"

Growing up is a very emotional process, and our children are frequently caught up in the powerful riptides of these emotions in a way that is difficult and often impossible for them to control. While we can look down from our seasoned perspectives and be very understanding, from the children's point of view, it can appear that they are failing simply because they can't control the flood of feelings.

Children look out at the world and see adults moving relatively effortlessly through life, all things under control, and definitely not buffeted by their emotions. Of course this is very far from a true picture, but we adults often consciously try to shield our children from our own emotional issues. From their vantage point, it looks as if adults are always in control.

Our children haven't yet learned fully how to manage the roiling white-water adventure of their emotions. Because it appears for all the world as if adults don't have this problem, it makes perfect sense for them to conclude that there is something wrong with them, that they are in some way inadequate. To counteract this tragic misconception, we need to report in regularly about our own feelings, so our children will see that having strong feelings is not a weakness, and that dealing with them appropriately is an ongoing part of life.

In *Emotional Intelligence*, Daniel Goleman revealed the importance of this previously neglected "kind of smart," which has a great deal to do with self-esteem and success in school and in life. One aspect of emotional intelligence is being aware of differing emotions and the ability to label them. When you share your feelings with a child, you teach them, not only that strong emotions are OK, but that they can be brought to consciousness, labeled, and dealt with. When we show our children our vulnerable true selves, it is easier for them to accept those parts of themselves and to open up and bare their souls.

Don't impose your feelings on them

Being open with our emotions around our children is important, but it is equally important to be very careful about which feelings we expose them to. We want to raise children who are comfortable in the world of emotions, who have learned the basic skills for navigating through their feelings. This means raising them in an environment where what we feel is as important and as regular a part of conversation as what we think. However, we can never lose track of the fact that, just as there are subjects that are not appropriate to discuss with children, there are emotions that are inappropriate to share as well.

Sometimes this is difficult to remember in the moment, particularly when we are going through an extended period of our own difficulties. Certainly, most emotional issues between spouses should not be shared with children. Not only are the emotions usually about issues that our children are far too young to understand, but they also put the children in a position of either directly or indirectly "taking sides," and that is something that no child should ever be asked to do. Additionally, serious emotional issues that are more appropriate for the ears of a therapist obviously should not be discussed in anything other than general terms. It is enough to explain that there is a problem and that it is being addressed responsibly.

Part of raising children with a healthy sense of self-esteem is making sure that, as adults, we keep the focus on who they are and what they need, not what we need from them. Far too many children are raised to be their parents' therapists and have the burden of coping with adult concerns before their own egos have fully developed.

Be aware of their fears and anxieties

Why does a five-year-old worry about his parents being seriously injured or killed? Why is a twelve-year-old suddenly obsessed by appearance? Why is a fourteen-year-old refusing to take part in gym class?

Being aware of the fears that children normally have at different developmental stages can help you cope much better with them yourself, as well as give you a leg up on helping to dispel those fears. It's natural for kids of kindergarten age to fear losing their parents, just as it's normal for sixth-graders to be very concerned with how they look, and eighth-graders to be self-conscious about changing clothes in front of others before gym class. Having fears is natural and healthy, but dealing with them appropriately is a skill children need to learn. If left to themselves, their fears can grow and become distorted out of all proportion, consuming time and energy that children should be putting toward learning and growing, making friends, and building up their own self-esteem.

One of the best ways to help children deal with their fears is to talk to them honestly and quietly. Fear is one of the few things that grow well in the dark, and by shining light on those fears, they can be shrunk down to a manageable size. This is relatively easy to accomplish when our children volunteer their fears, but our society has placed such a deep stigma on fearfulness that children get the message very early on that there is something "bad" or "weak" about being afraid. As a result, often the fears take root and grow in silence, and we need to pay careful attention to the nonverbal cues so that we can expose them to the light of language.

Make a loving public display

Why is it that the best things we say about our children we tend to say to others and in private? We brag about how great they did in the school play, we gush to confidantes about how well they are doing in school or sports, and then we go back and correct their English, and nag them about cleaning their rooms, getting to bed on time, and using proper table manners. We get so focused on our "job" of nudging, correcting, teaching, disciplining, and guiding that we forget to climb to the mountaintop and sing their praises as often and loudly as we can.

Sincere, heartfelt compliments and praise are always great confidence-boosters, and all the more so when they are publicly proclaimed. Sitting at the dinner table when friends or family are there, and hearing Mom or Dad telling everyone what a fabulous job a child did on a science project or how a child pulled off a major-league slide going into third base can be a powerful and deeply engraved event. Children know intuitively that, as the number of people present at a gathering increases, the relative importance of any one person there decreases. Therefore, when children are singled out and raised up to the crowd for approval, it can go a long way toward convincing them that they are indeed incredibly and uniquely special.

Of course, like anything else, this can be overdone. If you constantly point out your children's achievements to one and all, they may get the sense that they are only valued for what they can do, for their ability to give you "bragging rights" among parents. And don't forget to honor their privacy as well. Chances are there are some things they don't want to hear proclaimed publicly. Be sensitive to the content as well as the context of your praise!

Give them roots

Much of your child's sense of identity comes from you, and much of that depends on how good a job you do in giving them a strong foundation of family and ethnic pride. Much of that pride comes directly from the stories you tell.

We are a storytelling species. In a very important way, this is the crucial difference that separates us from the rest of the animal kingdom—we can remember, distill, and pass on information to the next generation, and the way we do it is through stories. Give your children a richly textured picture of where they come from—both personally and as part of an ethnic group. Connect them with your words to the places and people that preceded them. Help them see the ways that their heritage, their family history, and their cultural background can impact their lives.

When we give our children this kind of historical context, they develop a sense of roots, a sense that something solid, an irrefutable and indestructible beginning, is holding them up. This is important in the diverse society in which we live, where so many kids feel "less than," "ugly," or otherwise unacceptable because they do not fit the stereotype of the white middle class. Family and ethnic pride helps counteract those forces that demand that our children all look as if they came from the same cookie cutter. Such an exposure also helps them appreciate the ethnic roots of their friends and classmates, and helps break the destructive cycle of racism and self-hatred.

So tell them stories about their grandparents, their great-great-uncle, your own childhood; intersperse those with stories about what they were like when they were babies. Realize that they listen intently to what you say, whether they show you this or not, so invest your stories with as much pride and texture as you can. Not only will they love to hear these stories, the stories will help strengthen their sense of security and confidence in their own ability to forge connections in the world. They'll learn about the continuity of things, and they'll see their own future as part of that long line.

Accentuate the positive

When so much of raising a child is about teaching and challenging and setting boundaries, it is easy to get stuck in a mode of constant criticism. We notice all the mistakes, all the things not done that should have been done, all the irritating sloppy little "habits" our darlings have developed, and we almost can't stop ourselves from nagging, complaining, correcting, demanding, and snapping. It's a rare parent or teacher who never loses patience with the children under his or her wing. Most of us, try as we may, find ourselves short-tempered more often than we care to admit. If you feel your patience thinning and find that everything coming out of your mouth is negative, stop! It isn't going to help them, and it surely doesn't feel good to be reduced to being a constant complainer.

The truth is, the human brain is actually wired to track what works and to discard all else. Think of how babies learn to walk—they don't yell at themselves for falling down. They note what worked in the attempt and try again. Scientists label it "positive reinforcement." Whatever we call it, the more we can focus on what our children are doing right, the more we go with the natural patterns of the mind and help them notice what's right about themselves as well. Which, besides boosting esteem, goes a long way toward helping them adopt positive behaviors and drop negative ones.

Know when to be silent

Our children need to hear our words. They need to hear the delight in our voices when we are with them; they need to hear our pride and satisfaction when we talk about their accomplishments;

they need to hear the love, tenderness, and joy they bring out in us expressed in words. They need our empathy when they are hurting.

But, at the same time, our words must be sincere, consistent, and carefully used; they must ring with truth in order to be effective. And we need to remember that, sometimes, silence is golden.

If we hand out praise carelessly, we diminish its worth, and they will be the first to know. If we congratulate them on a job well done when they feel strongly that their effort was less than wonderful, we not only are ineffective in our attempt to make them feel better, we can do long-term damage by undermining our own credibility. If we gush on and on about something they feel is no big deal, we may undermine their sense of self-esteem by inferring that we don't think they are able to handle the hurt.

Words are powerful, and it is tempting, in our desire to strengthen our children's self-esteem, to lean heavily on the power of words to bolster and cement their sense of worth, importance, and competence. But we need to be very aware of the delicate balance between clearly articulating our love and pleasure in them, and sliding overboard into the dangerous territory where our words begin to have the opposite effect. Immoderate or insincere praise can not only undermine their self-esteem, but reduce us to bystanders whose words cannot be trusted.

Avoid sarcasm and teasing

Ah, teasing. I am an inveterate teaser. It's a way for me to show, in an indirect way, my feelings of love and connection to the person I'm teasing. But I have learned over the years from the girls and women in my life that my teasing is rarely received in the spirit in which it is offered. Perhaps it is a gender issue; in my experience, many more men are comfortable with teasing and sarcasm than women. Over and over, women tell me of the terrible wounds to their self-esteem they suffered as young girls from the teasing of, most often, their fathers and brothers. One woman I know goes as far as to claim that all teasing is a hostile act.

The problem with teasing, as I've come to see, is that the words meant in jest have nonetheless been spoken and, in some almost alchemical way, become real, even if they are meant to be harmless. A statement like, "You don't know anything about that, now do you?" is either a tease or a truth depending on tone of voice. But the words themselves are wounding, and often the tone is irrelevant to the listener. Also, because so many people have learned to hide their truth in teasing, teasers often do actually mean what they say, and therefore their words are intentionally hurtful.

Because teasing and sarcasm can so easily be misconstrued, if we are concerned with bolstering the self-esteem of the children in our care, it's probably best to avoid these modes altogether. If you find that difficult (as I do), at least be sensitive to the areas where children should never be teased—their looks (too loaded in this culture) and their competency (it's far too easy to reinforce insecurity). If it appears that you have hurt a child by your teasing, be sure to apologize and, if asked to stop, respect that boundary, rather than teasing the child about lacking a sense of humor.

Demonstrate respect

We can love them, we can lead by example, we can use the power of our words to bolster their confidence and encourage their efforts, but we must also show our children through our day-to-day actions that our love is not removed and our words are not hollow. Each day they are in our care, the actions we take or do not take demonstrate to the children in our lives that we have respect for them—or that we don't. Through careless actions, through putting down their choice of friends, of wardrobe, of books, or whatever, we send a strong message that we don't trust them to make wise choices, and that we don't respect the choices they make. This does immeasurable damage to self-esteem.

Our job as caretakers is to help our children learn to make good choices, and to affirm our belief in their ability to make wise choices. We do that, in part, by respecting, as much as possible, the choices they do make, and by demonstrating our deep respect for who they are as human beings. We show them through our patience and our willingness to tackle difficult issues like sexual harassment and abuse, which are violations of respect. We show them by listening deeply to what they have to say, even when it is not necessarily clearly articulated. We show them by trying mightily to understand the world as they experience it, even though we will always come up short. We show them by being willing to bend our schedules to make them our priority in the day-to-day unfolding of life. And we show them by walking the incredibly fine line between providing the safety and security they need to become fearless, and challenging them to stretch, grow, and think for themselves as often as possible.

6

Emotional Intelligence

One of the oldest and most revered jobs of a father is revealing the pathways to the future from which our children must
someday choose. Being their window on the world is a traditional role of fathers, but the character of what that means has
changed dramatically. However, as the world has become more
complex at an astonishing rate, what our children will inherit
is vastly more intricate and holds greater danger—as well as
greater possibilities—than even the world we grew up in just
a few short decades ago. Respecting the unique potential of
each of our children requires that we pay close attention to
this part of our job. Unfortunately for fathers, the single most
valuable skill our children need to succeed in their world is a
high degree of emotional sophistication, and, traditionally, this
is not a strength of men.

Become an emotional expert

For fathers, for men, it is difficult even to begin a discussion about emotions without bags full of extraneous trash getting in the way. It is unquestionably true that most men, for whatever reason and by whatever process, are much more emotionally reserved than most women. In general, it is more difficult for us to clearly identify, freely articulate, and comfortably admit to the broad spectrum of human emotions. It is also true (or at least it feels true) that most of us have, at one time or another, suffered under the brunt of a very emotionally charged accusation that all the problems of Western civilization have been caused by our own personal difficulty expressing our feelings. To put it mildly, emotions have become a very charged issue for men and, as uncomfortable as it may be, one that we must address head-on for the benefit of our children.

Ironically, in this often difficult undertaking of once again coming into full possession of our emotions, we are blessed with the best possible teachers—our children. Much of the time, children seem to run on little else but emotion. They cannot always accurately identify what they are feeling, but that is largely because they are so wrapped up in the feeling itself and they lack the vocabulary to articulate it. Helping our children identify, discuss, and respect their own feelings allows us to relearn the same lessons we may have misplaced somewhere along the journey.

In fact, parenting resembles nothing so much as a post-graduate degree in understanding and dealing with emotions. There are very few jobs imaginable for which the job description changes so radically over time. When our children are young, they assume that we know everything. From that lofty position, most of our energy can be focused on giving them the emotional support and encouragement they need—praising their efforts, listening to their ideas, creating opportunities for them to have some power, even if it's just over what's for dinner, what books to read, or which games to play. The heart of our attention is on their feelings, trying to help them understand and articulate the raw flood of emotions powering their little bodies.

As they grow older and begin to suspect that we aren't so smart after all, the balance begins to shift. As always, their feelings are the foundation from which we must begin, but increasingly, they will demand that we focus on the substance of things. This can be a very delicate dance, as their budding debating style sometimes veers into wildly illogical loops. We need to be skillful at honoring their feelings—dealing honestly and straightforwardly with their emerging intellect without making them feel foolish, and encouraging them to stretch their minds and souls farther outward.

Eventually, sometimes gradually and sometimes with jarring suddenness, we are bumped off the paternal pedestal. No matter how much we protest our fallibility, expose our stumblings, and apologize for our mistakes, the time comes when our children finally realize that we aren't the paragons of virtue and intelligence they once assumed we were. And when that time comes, they are frequently angry with us. It may feel unfair, and in some ways it undoubtedly is, but we can take comfort in the knowledge that it is an essential milestone in our children's initiation into adulthood. It is also the final transformation necessary to allow us to properly coach and counsel our young adults as they take their first tentative steps into the world of their own futures.

The easiest way to settle into this emotional university is just to spend time with our children without having to do anything, letting them know that they are important and they don't have to entertain us, they don't have to perform, they don't have to do anything but be themselves.

One way of reinforcing their certitude about that safety net of love is by becoming masters of empathy. It is a challenge that is surprisingly rewarding. True empathy goes beyond simply understanding how our children feel. It is the emotional discipline of taking yourself outside of time, putting yourself in the position that they now occupy, and then actually experiencing their feelings. It may be the simple but overwhelming frustration of your youngest child, who's always at the bottom of the pecking order. It may be the feeling of confused rejection after an argument with a best friend. It may be the feeling of being unfairly punished.

The range of our children's emotions is quite broad, but the span of our own emotional experiences is considerably broader. We have been there and beyond. We have had the same or similar experiences. It is not difficult to call upon our memories in order to place ourselves in proximity to their current position, and the benefits are extraordinary and immediate. When we experience their feelings, they cannot help but know it. And the better we get at sensing, decoding, and understanding the flow and texture of their emotions, the more they feel known, loved, safe, and secure.

When we are able to put ourselves in their place and feel what they are feeling, the rest is easy. Our children feel deeply understood and received. Our willingness to feel—rather than just understand—their feelings is both a demonstration of their importance to us and the proof of our love for them. Why, but for unfathomable love, would anyone want to reexperience the irrational anger, quivering fears, mind-numbing frustrations, heart-piercing anguish, and gut-wrenching sadness that comes with being a child?

The rewards of empathy are many. We can find ourselves standing comfortably side-by-side with our children—even when we are disciplining them. And we get to revisit all the emotional turmoil of our youth, but this time with the clarifying assistance of our adult perspective. It gives us the power to tame storms and quiet the rumbling insecurities of youth. At the same time, it heals us like a mythical mineral bath. You cannot do one without receiving the other.

Know that their emotions aren't all about you

One danger of being a student and teacher at the same time is that we can lose track of this point. "How could you do this to me?" How many times have you heard these words? How many times have you yourself said some variation of these words to your child? If you are like most people, the answer is more than you would like to admit. All of us sometimes slip into the self-centered position of thinking that everything is about us, but it is a very damaging role to assume, particularly when dealing with children who are struggling to understand and express their own feelings. When they stumble, act out, or get angry, we need to focus on their feelings, find out what is going on that has brought on this behavior.

By shifting the focus onto our own disappointment or anger at their behavior, we not only abandon them right at the moment they need us most to help them understand their motivation, we send them the dangerous message that their mistakes, their outbursts, are responsible for our pain. And by sending that message, whether we want to or not, we tell them to shut down emotionally.

Raising emotionally intelligent children means supporting them in the difficult and mistake-ridden journey through their emotions. To be their guide, we need the maturity and resilience to allow our own reactions to recede in importance. Even if their behavior is intended to upset us, as it sometimes is, our taking center stage as the injured party only reinforces our children's inappropriate way of expressing anger or frustration. It does nothing to help them figure out how to let us know more appropriately that they are upset with us about something.

Watch your body language, and theirs

Other than words, the way we communicate most often is through body language. Our words may hold meaning, but the way our bodies complement or contradict those words shows our true feelings. Through the way we sit, the way we gaze, our gestures, through every combination of physical poses possible, we shed light on our true feelings, and our children are masters at interpreting every nuance that we communicate.

Remember, from the time they were born, they have been studying us with an unbelievable intensity; knowing moods and our feelings is a central part of their job. Add to this the fact that, during the crucial formative years before they begin to master language, their focus is on how we communicate nonverbally, and it is easy to see how much information children pick up from even the most subtle shrugs, signs, or facial expressions. Like it or not, we are all open books to them.

So when we respond to their report of the day's activities by rotely saying "That's wonderful" without taking our eyes off the newspaper we are reading, the message we send isn't wonderful at all; it is terribly deflating. They know that, in that instant, reading the newspaper was more important to us than listening to them.

These are not subtle messages; they can be very damaging to a child's sense of self-importance and confidence, and unfortunately we can, and very often do, deliver them innocently and without even knowing we are doing it. After all, we're busy—how are we going to make dinner, catch up on the news, and pay attention to our children's concerns if we don't "multitask"?

Beyond that problem lies a more subtle one—our words and our body language must match up. If you say, "You're doing a great job," you have to mean it—with your smile, your encouraging eye contact. If you say one thing and demonstrate another with your body language, your children will pick up on the hypocrisy.

Talking to children about emotions can sometimes meet with a brick wall, but when we shift gears slightly and get them engaged in trying to interpret feelings from body language, it can become an engaging game with long-term benefits. Slumped shoulders, shuffling gait, scowls, leaning forward when someone is speaking, the movement of eyes, hands, and arms all may give us reliable information about how someone is feeling.

The more attuned children become to body language, the more the world of emotions is brought into their lives. It also gives them information that allows them to be more considerate and empathetic, and gives them a way to raise issues that might otherwise be difficult or awkward for them.

When using this technique, it's important to help kids understand that their guesses may be wrong. Not everyone does show their feelings in their bodies, so they need to learn both how to guess and how to check out their assumptions—for example, crossed arms may just be comfortable for someone and not necessarily mean they are hostile.

Listen well

Good listening skills are one of the most important prerequisites to caring for children. When they are infants, we need to hone our ears to be able to decipher the cranky cry from the wet cry from the scared cry. As they grow, we need to learn how to hear the meaning behind their words. As they struggle with both the depth and difficulty of language and the much more complicated job of trying to translate what they feel into words that adequately convey their meaning, we need to be their receptive interpreters.

Children who are listened to learn to speak earlier and are more socially outgoing and confident as the years go by. Yet at times, it's hard to keep it all in perspective, simply because children have such an extraordinary capacity to go on and on. Of course our energy wanes, and we find it difficult to be 100 percent attentive all the time, but we need to give it our best effort.

Chatter about the robot made today in preschool or the new girl on the bus are very important in your child's life. When we do our best to answer our children's barrage of questions, we reinforce their sense of self-worth. If we listen well, they know that their opinions and feelings are being taken seriously, and hence they feel valued.

Young children often don't know how to talk about their feelings, so part of "listening" to young kids is helping them put what they feel or think into words. So be attentive, look for clues from body language, be sensitive to what they may be leaving out. Children whose age is in the double digits (ten and older) should be pretty articulate about what they are feeling. It is important to let kids this age and older have the time to talk out their ideas and problems. Try not to interrupt, put words into their mouths, or talk too much. To show you are listening, stay in the conversation by occasionally recapping a conclusion your child has made, using different words.

Practice seeing the world through their eyes

The one thing we all want more than anything else is to be understood for who we really are—such a simple thing, and yet seemingly so incredibly elusive. One of the great opportunities we are given as parents is to provide exactly that to our children—understanding. And it is precisely in the employment of this magic that we can have our most powerful effect on our children. The irony is that understanding them can be difficult.

For most of us, this has come as something of a surprise. For some reason, we seem to assume that understanding our children will come naturally. Maybe we assume they'll be a lot like us, or at least that our careful nurturing will go a long way toward "molding" them into who they are. It is, therefore, often a shock to find out that your sweet little child has its own and very different set of needs, curiosities, and interests. On the one hand, it's astounding to realize that such a tiny person can come so fully equipped with all the ingredients of a full-blown unique personality. But at the same time, it means we now have to work (and sometimes work hard) to understand them with the depth they deserve.

The first part of the challenge is to drop all our preconceived ideas. We have to stop assuming, and instead watch and wonder. Listen to the things they talk about and that interest them. Try to track the threads that tie their youthful, wandering thoughts together. Dig deeply into the whys and wherefores of their feelings. Try to remember what you were like at their age; try to imagine what it must be like to be a child in this day and age.

Fit yourself in their shoes as snugly and often as you can and leave yourself open to who they really are. Chances are, you will find traits you'd rather not find—maybe your son has a hair-trigger temper, or your daughter procrastinates and loves to play with spiders, or wants to be a police officer when she grows up. These may not be your preferences, but then, it isn't your life either. Accept it, make your peace, and get on with the much more important job of knowing them deeply and loving them for all the uniqueness they bring to the world.

Work through the silence

One of the most difficult bumps in the road for parents is when, all of a sudden, their sons or daughters retreat into silence. The reasons can range from those that are minor and may easily be addressed to much more serious ones, and it is not always easy to figure out—especially since they aren't talking. The one thing we know for sure is that they have withdrawn from us, and that in itself is a problem.

The reason may be as simple as a feeling that they are not good at verbalizing. Everyone has different communication styles, but this problem can come up easily in a quiet child in a family dominated by big-time talkers. And it often initiates a vicious spiral downward. Maybe dad and older sister love to engage in spirited verbal battles at the dinner table, and younger daughter feels completely outmatched. That starts her feeling inadequate, then down goes the self-esteem, and soon she is convinced she can't even express herself well, so why even try.

It can also be a sign of more serious issues, particularly if a family hasn't been communicating well for a while. Your son may be grappling with a serious issue and feeling isolated, un-supported, and as if he doesn't have anyone he can trust or in whom he can confide. Whatever the reason, the severance of communication is a signal that can't be ignored.

The first thing we need to do is reflect deeply on our own role in creating this breach. All too often, their silence is a red flag trying to warn us that we have not been doing out job well enough. Once we have some idea of why we have been cut off, we can begin to repair the breach. But it must be done slowly and with extraordinary sensitivity. The last thing you want to do at this point is to force a confrontation that just ends up making them more defensive. Instead, you need to show them that you respect their decision to withdraw—temporarily—and offer them other ways of expressing themselves and other people with whom they may find it easier to talk. Affirm your love and willingness to go through anything with them.

Pay special attention to your sons

Big boys don't cry; they grow up to be men who have precious little understanding of their own emotional centers. This is the signature statement of how we have raised our sons for centuries. And in denying them their tears, we have unwittingly cut them off at a very tender age from the entire world of healthy emotions. That is a handicap even more devastating in its effects than losing one's sight or hearing, for only our feelings can lead us to the essential truth about ourselves.

When we raise our sons without access to their emotions, we deny them the whisper of their deepest wisdom. Within the incredibly intricate, complex, and confusing path of life, this capacity for knowing is our greatest gift. Yet instead of nurturing this gift and training our boys in its use, we have largely allowed it to wither and recede into the background.

Without access to this miraculous tool, our sons grow up like carpenters without saws, trying to fit all the pieces of their lives together without the ability to cut, shape, and size the materials they are given. They operate by someone else's design, and the results can only be the construction of a life that does not reflect who they truly are.

Don't guess, ask

Communicating love in a way our sons can receive it is not always easy, because we don't always know what they want and it never occurs to them to tell us. The range of things that can mean love is as broad and varied as our imaginations. It may be hugs, special gifts, appreciative notes. It may be praise, but maybe only praise about certain things. It may be time together doing nothing. It may be the quiet sharing of stories, thoughts, and feelings; it may be reading together, playing together, taking walks together.

The possibilities are endless, so ask. Otherwise, you may never learn. Be specific and keep asking until you get an answer. Then keep asking again and again as they grow, for just like you, their needs and wants change. Put what you have learned into practice, but, at the same time, don't overdo it. Communicating love is a precious act and should be done often, but not routinely. The honesty and specialness of the moment must be preserved.

Teach the language of emotion

Our language is rich in words of emotion, but if you ask most people to start listing words that describe feelings, they rattle off a half-dozen or so—angry, sad, disappointed, frustrated, happy, joyful—and, yes, they almost always start with the negative ones and grind to a halt. So review the partial list below and think about times you had these feelings. Then start today to expand your own emotional vocabulary.

Safe, relaxed, satisfied, undesirable, lethargic, needy, confident, optimistic, loved, insulted, resentful, ignored, excited, energized, connected, empty, trapped, obligated, amused, fortunate, effective, rotten, infuriated, idiotic, empowered, spirited, peaceful, puzzled, resigned, terrified, special, wonderful, vibrant, regretful, intolerant, gullible, respected, fantastic, elated, hesitant, horrible, hated, eager, excellent, engaged, indifferent, inept, invisible, tremendous, tipsy, tingly, lonely, lousy, lost, forgiven, funny, fearless, grumpy, guilty, gullible, enthusiastic, enriched.

Respect their feelings

Sounds simple, but it isn't. Their feelings are exactly that—their feelings. They are real, they are true, and they are a precious gift when shared. But they can also be difficult to hear without becoming defensive ourselves, so we need to resist pulling out all the tricks we have developed over time to deflect and negate the feeling.

Just as an example, your son says to you, "You don't love me!" It's absurd, and our automatic response system wants to kick in with "Don't even say that" or "Of course I love you" or "That's ridiculous." But each of those answers sends the same message in differing degrees: "Your feelings are wrong or stupid." And in that moment, you are the one who is wrong, because you completely ignore what he is feeling and jump instantly to your own defense. In the process, you send the more damning message that you don't want to hear about his feelings.

Feelings are never wrong; they simply are. They may emerge from a misunderstanding or a failure to properly communicate, and at times they can be inappropriate or misplaced, but they are always true. We need not only to treat them with respect, but to be thankful that, in this one place in our lives, we can always know that the truth is being spoken.

Respond to feelings first

Respecting our children's feelings is the start; responding immediately is the next step. Getting our children to express their feelings is difficult enough; the very least we can do is be meticulously careful to respond immediately and compassionately to them when they are offered. Surprisingly, many adults stumble over this, with potentially devastating results, particularly with their sons.

Often, when boys do get up the courage to express their emotions, it is because the feelings are so strong they simply have to come out. In many of those situations, the feelings are not well articulated and not at all what we want to hear. Our job is to sift through all the accusing or hostile words, find the core feelings, and articulate them back whether we like them or not.

When your son tells you, "You never listen to me!" what he is really saying is that "my experience is that you don't really listen to what I am trying to say, and that hurts." The issue you need to deal with first and foremost is his feeling that he is hurt. Address the feeling before going on to the issue that may have provoked the feelings.

Teach them to take responsibility for their feelings

We are so poorly trained in the language of emotions that, even when we use the right words, we rush past the feeling to assign blame for the "creator" of that feeling. "You hurt my feelings!" After all, if I feel hurt, then certainly someone must have made me feel this way! What gets lost in the presumptuous conclusion is everything of any substance. In the first place, more often than not, the person being accused of "making you feel hurt" never had any intention of hurting you. They may have said something or done something that they should have known might hurt you, but simply didn't think of the consequences. Then again, they may have done or said something that they had no idea would hurt you. It is rare indeed that they purposefully tried to hurt you, yet that is the stinging message they receive back.

In the second place, remarkable as it sounds, no one can "make you" feel anything. Your emotional response is your own responsibility—what angers one person may embarrass or even please another. One significant component of emotional intelligence is taking responsibility for our own feelings. Help your children learn the difference between how they feel and what, in fact, has happened.

Most of us were never taught about the arena that social scientists call "managing feelings." What they mean by this is not "management" in the traditional male mode of repression and denial. Rather, they mean knowing what to do about strong emotions. Do you collapse in tears? Allow the feeling to move through you? Tell the other person? Seek help from others? Decide to distract yourself instead?

The truth is that all of these (and many other) choices are appropriate under different circumstances, and yet many of us aren't even consciously aware that we have any choice at all! The first thing we can do is let our sons know that there is a variety of healthy responses to feelings, and give them a list: Write a letter you never send expressing how you feel; act out your feeling with your body; go into a room alone and scream at the top of your lungs; take your feeling for a walk alone; call a friend and ask him or her to listen without saying anything.

We can't help our children feel the full spectrum and intensity of their emotions without giving them some tools to deal with them.

Allow them to express themselves in their own way

We live in a world that values words, preferably expressed in a calm, rational manner. There is much to be said for that ability, but we can get so focused on channeling all our children's energy into that one narrow outlet that we dampen and miss out on other expressive ways of communicating with us. When they come running up to us talking a mile a minute, hands flying all over the place, excitedly pacing or rocking, or maybe dragging their feet and hanging their head, resist the temptation to get them to cut to the chase, and "tell you" what's up.

Stop for a moment and observe the way they are expressing their feelings. Often, particularly when they sink into a noncommunicative phase, this will be the only evidence you have of what is really going on inside them. Become a master of interpreting clues that can reveal the feelings they may or may not be willing or ready to express. Celebrate their expressiveness, because it can help you understand them better and because it is a natural part of their own fledgling attempts to let their feelings show.

Play with feelings

Children play, thank goodness, or we would never get anything done! But children's play has a point; they are practicing all kinds of emotional, social, and intellectual skills. We have long known that children's play prepares them for the different stages of their lives, but we have been slow to turn this wonderful laboratory to its best use. In a sense, we allow our children to dictate how, when, and what they will play. Some of that is good, in that it can allow their own creative needs to be met. But we need to start paying attention to their play and participate, both in the play itself and in the direction it takes.

More and more frequently, we abdicate this fertile ground to the television. Children are easily captured by stunning visual images, whether it be Barney or the Power Rangers, and their play takes on a decidedly directed and sometimes unhealthy bent. One area that is almost completely neglected is playing at emotions. If we want our boys to grow up in touch with and in control of the emotions within them, it would help if we gave them some early practice through play. There are at least two components of emotional intelligence that kids can learn through play. One is to identify the feeling: I'm mad; I'm frustrated; I'm excited. The other is what to do about the feeling: I'm going home; I'm going to tell you how I'm feeling; I'm taking a walk.

Give their feelings room

Despite all the sweet talk about caring and concern for each other's feelings, most people are incredibly bad at demonstrating care and concern in the moment. We gravitate to our own feelings, latch onto them like a life vest in a turbulent sea, and completely disregard how the other person is feeling. That's why so many disagreements end up with us figuratively curled up in the fetal position in our own corner, astonished at the lack of love and concern being displayed by our partners.

Such behavior makes for a rocky and ultimately distant relationship, but the one place we have absolutely no right to behave in such a juvenile manner is with our children. The rule of thumb when dealing with our kids is that it is their feelings that matter, not ours. We are supposed to be the adults, the guides who will help them understand and navigate this difficult world. We can't do that unless we put all the focus in the right place. They will undoubtedly do things that hurt us, that disappoint us, that make us angry, and they need to know it when they do, but not until we have effectively explored their emotional experience.

When kids are faced with parental volatility, one of two things happens: either they learn to become hysterical themselves to get attention, or they shut down altogether because there isn't any space for them to experience and express their own emotional reaction—they're too busy trying to avoid yours. Both can have serious consequences, although the behavior of a hysterical child is more overt. I once knew an adolescent who didn't tell his mom he was being molested for a year because he didn't want to deal with her hysteria.

Help them to grieve

Emotions exist for a reason: to be experienced so that we can learn more about the deeper parts of ourselves. When we shut that experience down, we not only turn our backs on vital information that could enrich our lives beyond imagination, we also build a wall around a part of our inner being, a wall that blocks us from conscious understanding. The more often we do this, the less access we have to the very information we need to live our lives consciously. After years of repressing emotions, our interior landscape becomes a clutter of unknown obstacles, and our conscious decisions start to drift into shallow parody, cut off from any real information about who we are and what we need.

The stronger the emotion repressed, the more damage we do to ourselves, and it is hard to imagine an emotion more powerful than grief. Yet, the very power of that feeling often stops us in our tracks. We know intuitively that to experience grief truly may mean losing control, collapsing in a sobbing fit of tears that feels for all the world like a never-ending spiral into despair. If we are lucky, we learn that experiencing grief, in all its painful intensity, does not harm, but heals, us and ultimately deepens our understanding and appreciation of life itself. It is a lesson that is very difficult for children to learn on their own, but it is a gift of extraordinary importance that we can offer them.

Teach the difference between feeling and acting

One of the hallmarks of emotional intelligence is impulse control; thinking before acting. Like other aspects of emotional "smarts," children tend to have trouble with this. Of course, it can get them into all kinds of trouble when young, and if not learned, it can lead to difficulties with drugs, alcohol, and violence later in life.

A key component of impulse control is to understand the difference between feelings and actions. Just because you feel something doesn't mean you should act on it, and understanding that truth goes a long way toward creating good impulse control.

Help your children understand that feelings exist outside our conscious control. They just are; they arise and fall in an ongoing flow: frustration, elation, sadness, anger, hurt, joy. They get triggered in us by the intersection of the outside world with our personal histories. That's why the same thing that can make you cry may have no effect on me. We have different life circumstances.

Whether or not to act on a feeling—to tell someone you're mad or to stomp off in a huff, for example—is a choice. You don't actually have to act on any feeling. Sometimes it's better not to. We need to teach our children that just because they feel something doesn't mean they have to do anything about it. What's best is to notice the feeling first, identify it, and then think about whether acting on it is a good idea.

Cultivate emotional insight

Insight is yet another dimension to emotional intelligence. Insight is the capacity to perceive the nature of something. Emotional insight allows us to identify patterns in our emotional reactions and, perceiving the patterns, have more choices in our reactions.

Instead of just freaking out, for example, every time you see a big dog coming down the street, treating it as a random and isolated event, look for a pattern. With this insight, you are able to think, "Oh, I guess I'm afraid of big dogs. I see I do this every time one comes along." Once you have that awareness, the pattern has less effect on you. The next time a big dog comes along, you can think to yourself, "Here's that thing again that scares me." Recognizing that often helps alleviate some of the panic. With maturity, you can even go further and analyze why you are afraid and what other choices you have as to how to react.

People without emotional insight go through life as if every day were their first day on the Earth, making the same mistakes again and again and never realizing them, much less taking responsibility for them. I once had a friend who had been married four times—twice to an alcoholic, once to a gambler, and once to a compulsive eater. When I asked her if she saw a pattern to her relationships, she looked at me dumbfounded. Until she could see her attraction to addicts, she would continue to pick addicts to marry.

Insight allows us to learn from our emotional mistakes and to correct them. Help your boy begin to thread together the emotional patterns of his life.

Make home a haven

The world can be a scary place. It's hard enough when we are all grown up and have to try to make sense out of things and find our place and purpose in the midst of all that clatter and confusion. Just imagine how alternately beautiful and wondrous and mysteriously terrifying it can be to a child without any of the resources necessary to sort it out. Yet that is the world we are raising them to live in. Therein lies one of the greatest challenges we face as caregivers—how to protect our children adequately, to shield them from the full harshness of the world, while at the same time preparing them fully to deal with the world as it truly is. It's a difficult balancing act. One of the key pieces that we can put in place without having to worry about whether we are overdoing it is to create a safe, secure, and supportive haven for them at home.

One part of that formula entails the conscientious elimination of any residual tensions. If you have an argument, if for any reason you need to discipline them, if there are any lingering issues between you that make your interactions uncomfortable, then you need to resolve them as quickly, compassionately, and supportively as possible. Get through the issues and back to what is important—your love and support for them—as quickly as possible. Home is no place for tension, uncertainty, or bad feelings. Without a solid foundation on which to build, it will be difficult for them to believe there is anything they can count on.

A second part of that formula is to try to help them make their own space within your home—one that supports, nourishes, and reflects their emerging identity. This can require some tongue-biting at times, since the likelihood of your decorating ideas matching theirs is pretty slim. But remember, this is their inner sanctum, the place they need to feel most comfortable, so go out of your way to be helpful and supportive.

Respect their privacy

One day, your children are crawling all over you, chattering away a mile a minute about the intricate details of their day, and then it seems the very next day, they become secretive and concerned about privacy. As they grow, they naturally begin to separate their lives from yours. That much we can understand in theory, since the whole idea is to see them off into their own lives fully capable and confident in their own abilities.

But the process can be difficult to endure. It usually takes place in fits and starts; one day we are confidantes; and the next day we are excluded. Even very young children who have just reached school age may be reluctant to share information with us about their new world, and the need for privacy only increases through high school. While it can be hard, particularly with a child who used to share everything, we must honor their need to experience and experiment with secrets and privacy, because ultimately, they are practicing exercising their own judgment about what is theirs alone and what and who will have access to different parts of their lives. In other words, we may not like being excluded, but they are practicing becoming strong, self-reliant, and self-confident.

Show your respect for their efforts by allowing them the privacy they desire. Allow them to designate which parts of their room or drawers in their desk are off-limits to others. Support them if snooping siblings invade their domain, and, unless you have a very good reason (grave emotional and bodily harm), discipline yourself to keep out of their private space.

Teach them how to think for themselves

It's easy to think that care-giving means bossing around the children in our lives. After all, they know nothing (at least in the beginning), and by now, we know a great deal, so it is natural to assume that parenting is a process of telling what we know. But that tendency is dead wrong. Most of what kids learn they must experience for themselves, and to the extent they do comply with our advice, they are in danger of becoming kids with low self-esteem who can't make an independent decision.

Teaching something to someone is not about telling them where to look when they swing or where to put their feet or what to do and not to do. Rather, it is placing the learner in the environment and asking the right questions so that the learner can experience it for themselves. Coaching therefore becomes more of a process of inquiry than a lecture.

Parenting and teaching are very much like coaching. The more we can avoid the tendency to speechify and instead ask our children good questions when they come to us for advice or in the context of a conversation, the more they will actually create the inner framework for making healthy decisions in their own lives.

Instead of lecturing them when they do something wrong, ask them to reflect on the consequences: "When you hit Francine, what happened? How did you feel? How did she feel? What did you learn from that?" Instead of giving a lecture on good study habits, have them experiment with a couple of methods and then follow up with questions: "Do you do better on a multiple-choice test when you read the book two days before and then have a conversation with someone about it, or does it help more to take a walk first, and then review at the last minute?" The more our children understand themselves, how they learn, and how they feel, the more they can make their way easily in the world, brimming with the confidence such knowledge imparts.

Show your love in a way they can receive it

Loving our children is easy; figuring out how to communicate that love is more difficult; and doing it on a consistent basis is more difficult still. Part of the problem stems from our own unarticulated sense that with a love so strong, somehow the children should just "know." They don't, and the ways they can receive love will change over time. Sometimes, when they are young and still unspoiled by the traps our culture sets for them, the words themselves are enough. Often, as they get older and are struggling with the different images of what they are supposed to be, our children need more than words; they need us to do something that can only come from our love for them. It could be simply talking to them, without lecturing and with our heart wide open. It could be taking time out of our busy schedule to spend with them. It could be sharing something special with them and them alone.

What works will shift and change over time, and it is our responsibility to shift and change with it. It is our responsibility to remind our children on a regular basis both how precious they are to us and how important it is never to stop communicating that love. Both messages are crucial, because our children need every ounce of our love to give them the strength and courage to grow into emotionally healthy individuals. Parents who model for their children the ability and importance not only of maintaining that strong emotional connection but communicating it regularly are the best examples they will ever have.

Do things together

There is an old adage that says, "Men do, women are." Like most gender assumptions, there is a kernel of truth to this. Much more than with our daughters, with whom we can have a conversation about feelings, if we want a freely flowing emotional connection to our sons, in which we can freely explore their feelings, we need to *do* things with them on a regular basis.

Traditionally, boys build their emotional connections to others through activities. Whether this is a genetic predisposition or simply centuries-old learned behavior will undoubtedly remain unclear for years, but the consequences are clear: boys generally connect with others most easily by doing things together.

And we need to be the ones who initiate the doing. Because of old, but still powerful, stereotypes, boys are both less ready to articulate emotional disappointment and more willing to act "tough" by accepting your lack of participation without complaint. It may seem a small thing, but the combination of culturally induced resistance to discussing feelings and the equally strong cultural admonition to be "strong" can create gaping holes of disconnection that our boys fall into easily and do not know how to escape.

With today's accelerated pace, it may be difficult, but find a way to do something with your children on a daily basis. After all, in the final analysis few things will ever be as important as your children. Live that importance by remembering that what we want to do and what our intentions are do not matter nearly as much as what we actually do.

To Our Readers

Conari Press, an imprint of Red Wheel/Weiser, publishes books on topics ranging from spirituality, personal growth, and relationships to women's issues, parenting, and social issues. Our mission is to publish quality books that will make a difference in people's lives—how we feel about ourselves and how we relate to one another. We value integrity, compassion, and receptivity, both in the books we publish and in the way we do business.

Our readers are our most important resource, and we value your input, suggestions, and ideas about what you would like to see published. Please feel free to contact us, to request our latest book catalog, or to be added to our mailing list.

Conari Press

An imprint of Red Wheel/Weiser, LLC

500 Third Street, Suite 230

San Francisco, CA 94107

www.redwheelweiser.com